In praise of *Funding Happiness*

'Funding Happiness is a refreshing and insightful read that puts people, not products, at the heart of financial planning. It captures the essence of what great financial planning is all about – helping people clarify what truly matters to them and building a financial strategy that supports those aspirations. As a profession, we have a responsibility to move the conversation away from purely numbers and investments, and towards life goals, wellbeing, and purpose. This book shines a light on that shift and will inspire both advisers and clients alike.'
— Carla Brown, President, Personal Finance Society

'Advisers and their clients will welcome an evidence-based handbook on financial planning. Ben Goss and his Dynamic Planner team have created a practical guide to the nexus between money and happiness. Advisers who give this reader-friendly book to their clients will be empowered to build deeper and more valuable relationships with them.'
— Danby Bloch, Author and Head of Editorial Strategy at Platforum

'A valuable resource of financial education and empowerment for advisers to share!

The balance between risk and reward is a foundation of the financial planning process and Funding Happiness offers an engaging exploration of the dilemma faced by all investors, whilst underlining the value of professional financial advice.

This is a great resource for advisers to share with clients, to help build their knowledge and confidence to take the next step in their financial journey.'
— Keith Richards, CEO, Consumer Duty Alliance

I can't think of a better guide to the world of financial planning and investing than Ben Goss. Drawing on years of accumulated wisdom, this compulsively readable book is the perfect primer for anyone who wants greater control over their money. If you've ever worried about financing your future, this is the place to start.
— Tom Browne, Editor of Money Marketing

What Ben has given the industry with Funding Happiness is an easy to read and understand primer on how financial planning works and why investors should use the acumen and experience of financial advisers to help them manage their financial road ahead.

Any existing or potential financial advice client who reads this book will have not only a clear understanding of the whats, whys and wherefores of the financial advice process but a confidence that using a financial adviser can be in their best interests in helping them manage and grow their wealth, in short, funding their happiness.
— Rob Kingsbury, Consulting Editor, Professional Paraplanner

Thank you to Ben for creating such a meaningful and practical resource. This book will help inspire young people to take control of their financial futures and build lives with stability and purpose.

Financial knowledge is more than just what you are earning; it's about understanding how to use it to shape the life you've always imagined, and this book is a powerful resource in helping people do exactly that.

Funding Happiness breaks down and gives an accessible framework, especially to young people embarking on a social mobility journey understanding risks and giving the confidence and tools to make informed decisions about their futures. It goes beyond traditional financial advice, encouraging readers to think about purpose, wellbeing, and long-term impact.

At Urban Synergy, we are committed to helping young people thrive in education and careers, and resources like this play an important role in supporting that journey.
— Leila Thomas, CEO & Founder of Urban Synergy Youth Empowerment & Social Mobility Charity

Funding Happiness

How to fund the life you want at a risk that's right for you

Ben Goss

First published in Great Britain in 2026

Design, typesetting and publishing by UK Book Publishing.

www.ukbookpublishing.com

ISBN: 978-1-918077-51-3

Contents

Introduction

The dilemma

Stephen and Sarah

One Sunday evening, Stephen and Sarah were sitting at their living room table with the television muted in the background and a laptop open in front of them. They were both staring blankly at the screen, trying to find the right words.

Why is this so difficult?
Why can't we talk about it sensibly?
Surely it's too risky?

They had stopped looking at each other, desperate to avoid the escalation they knew could easily happen.

Stephen's statement had been one of the biggest of their lives together. After 25 years of marriage, two children, successful careers and lots of ups and downs along the way, it felt like it had come out of the blue.

Sarah – a maths teacher, now head of year at the local senior school – loved numbers; she loved logic, she *needed* logic. Stephen – the creative director in his graphic design business, which he had built up over 20 years – did not. Stephen loved design, art, music, emotion – anything but numbers. He had a finance director in the business for that. Stephen could also be quite impulsive. The differences that made their marriage work, that made it interesting and varied, often came between them when money was involved.

But Stephen had made up his mind, or so he said.

The next few minutes, days, weeks would be crucial to ensuring a happy life together. Or perhaps they would break them.

'I'm not happy,' Stephen had said as he sat down. 'I want to sell the business and stop working.'

'You can't!' Sarah reacted, almost on autopilot. 'You know we can't afford it. We have the mortgage, the kids' university costs – they'll be on the family payroll for years. Have you seen the grocery bill recently, or the electric? Even though I've got the head of year job now, my salary barely touches the sides. Did you look at the spreadsheet I made?'

'Yes, but I'm unhappy. I'm unfulfilled and I always promised myself I would stop when I felt this way. You know I want to travel more, to give back. Spend more time volunteering overseas, like we did when we first met. Look at our pensions,' said Stephen, pointing to the laptop. 'We can afford it.'

'So you want to stop working, travel more and leave home – great! What about me? What about our commitments?' Sarah felt hurt and unheard. She also felt scared. When she was a child, her family had had a financial shock when her father's business failed. Money became very tight, and her parents eventually divorced. Although she was desperate to avoid reacting in the moment, she felt compelled to point to what she saw as the flaws and risks in what Stephen had said.

And so they now sat in silence, each trying to work out where to go next in this conversation they both knew was important but neither was prepared for.

Aisha

That same night, Aisha was sitting up in bed, scrolling on her phone and chatting with an AI. Next to her lay Sammy, her six-year-old son, out for the count in his pyjamas after being read three chapters, not the usual two, of his favourite adventure story. Aisha was exhausted and longed to sleep, but she was troubled as she looked at her bank balance, checked her savings account and got the AI to do some maths.

She had to work in the morning, but that gnawing feeling wouldn't leave her.

How can I ever afford it?
How do other people do it?
Surely it can't be that risky?

A successful project manager in a manufacturing firm, Aisha was desperate to move out of her rented flat and buy a house: a small place she and Sammy could truly call their own, with a garden he could run around and play football in. More than that, though, Aisha was desperate to spend more time with her boy. In the morning, she would drop him off at the childminder's for the day before getting the bus into work. Although she only worked three days a week in the office, those days seemed to drag on forever. Sammy was getting older, and she missed him. Aisha had been well trained at her current company, and she felt sure she could make a go of freelancing. She would only have to work half the time she did in her current job to make the same money at contractor rates. She could also work from home most of the time – and that's what she really wanted: that's what would really make her happy.

But how to do it all? A mortgage would require an income. She felt sure she could replicate her income as a contractor – the AI said she should be able to – but what about her pension and other benefits? As a single mum, she was entirely responsible for Sammy herself. Looking after him and making sure he was safe was her first priority. Nonetheless, it was a risk she was willing to take – a risk she *wanted* to take – but she really wanted some help. In truth, she had been thinking about this for months, but had never quite put it to the top of her list.

Aisha put down her phone, turned the bedside light off and fell asleep, too tired to think any more.

George

Earlier that same Sunday, George, a retired GP, had finished mowing the lawn and pruning the hedges at the back of his four-bedroom house. He now sat at his garden table drinking a cup of tea, listening to the birds and admiring his handywork. Originally from the Caribbean,

George took any chance he could get to sit outside and enjoy the sunshine. This was his family home and, although his daughter had moved out long ago and George was on his own as a widower, he loved the place. The trees he'd planted with his wife, the wildflower garden they'd cultivated together, the spaces inside and out where his daughter had played: the house and garden were full of happy memories. He was also mortgage free, which was a source of great comfort to him. He hoped to leave the property to his daughter.

On the table in front of him were the Sunday papers. George turned to the Money section. In his early seventies and retired for five years now, he lived off his pensions and savings, which he had built up steadily over his career. He liked to do his own research and keep abreast of the markets – but it was becoming more and more of a chore, and he increasingly kept his money in the bank. The headlines shouted: 'Top investment performers of the year', 'How to maximise income and beat inflation', 'Six tips to save you tax today'. *Not today*, thought George, and turned to the travel pages instead. He was planning a trip to Australia later in the year to see his daughter and grandchildren for a whole month. It was a trip he made every year. As he got older, the distance, the cost and, increasingly, the carbon footprint bothered him, but it was worth it, he told himself: it made him very happy. An article on sustainable tours to the Great Barrier Reef caught his eye, but as he read it, he couldn't help wondering:

Am I taking too much risk?
Is my money doing more harm than good to the planet?
Could I run out of money?

George fully expected to live a long life, just like his parents before him, but while he had a good pension, he was eating into his savings pretty regularly now – 'melting the iceberg' as his friends at the golf club called it, what with the big house, long-haul travel and the price of seemingly everything rising. As he packed up to walk back inside for the evening, he thought, *I really must make sure my money lasts*.

A very human problem

The dilemmas faced by Stephen and Sarah, Aisha and George are shared by millions of others up and down the country—and, indeed, around the world. These dilemmas keep us awake at night because we are pulled in two directions at once. As humans, we are 'wanting animals'—we want the best for ourselves and our loved ones—but we are also risk averse. So much so, in fact, that we dislike losing money more than twice as much as we like making it. Hundreds of thousands of years of human conditioning, where we avoid putting ourselves in dangerous situations that we may not survive, are deeply embedded in our brains. This conditioning runs contrary to our desire to better ourselves, to want more.

This leaves us with a peculiarly human problem: the need to accept some level of risk and discomfort now for success and happiness later. But how much risk? How much discomfort? Well, that depends a great deal on what you want and what will make you happy in the future. The trade-off is not easy, but it can be done.

And that's where a financial adviser comes in.

It often takes an outsider—someone who can be trusted, and who has the training and experience to ask the right questions, in the right order—to help us stand back and understand our options. Someone to give us the confidence to do something we have evolved over millennia not to do.

Why read this book?

THE VALUE OF ADVICE

'A few years ago I asked a couple what "good" looked like with their life and wealth. The husband said, "Selling my business for the highest price." The wife responded, "Getting my husband and our children's father back from his business so we can enjoy life together."'

Chances are, this book has been recommended to you by your financial adviser, or one you are considering working with. Or perhaps you are thinking about your long-term finances and reflecting on whether you should work with an adviser at all?

Either way, advisers know that the better informed you are about the principles and concepts that underpin financial advice, the easier, more enjoyable and more productive your relationship will be. Advisers see people like Stephen and Sarah, Aisha and George all the time. They know the right questions to ask, and they're used to listening to your answers and helping guide you towards the right choices.

Advisers also know that while they can guide you in the time you have together, ultimately your success is down to you: to your commitment to the life you want to fund, to your understanding of why that life is important to you, and to your commitment to the strategies and actions you agree together.

This book is designed to do three things for you as you work with your financial adviser:

1. Provide clarity on what actually makes you and your loved ones happy, and therefore what needs to be funded.

2. Give you more confidence in engaging with your long-term finances, so you can work more productively with your adviser.

3. Help you fund the life you want, at a risk that's right for you and the planet.

Why trust this book?

I wrote this book because I want to pass on what my colleagues and I have learned over the last 20-plus years from building the UK's most widely used digital advice platform.

When we started our company back in 2003, Dynamic Planner was looked at as a bit of an oddity. 'Why would I use this with my clients?' asked one financial adviser. 'I have this,' he said, holding up a pen, 'and this,' showing me the back of envelope.

Dynamic Planner, then as now, is designed to incorporate the methods used by major institutions to manage money and risk. These are methods refined over half a century to ensure those institutions can make money over the long term, in good markets and bad, at a level of risk that's right for them. We called it 'Dynamic' because we knew that, as human beings, we are not wired to focus on the long term. We knew that to help advisers engage people in the subject of their finances, we needed something that built a *dynamic* picture of the future and assessed the level of risk they were willing to take to achieve it.

More than 20 years on, almost half of UK financial advice firms now use Dynamic Planner – and to date they've put it to work for more than two million people like you. It's been designed, tested and refined with leading researchers, with many academic papers published for independent scrutiny, and it's even been used by the industry's regulator to assess the risk of investment portfolios.[1] Its launch was seen as revolutionary at the time[2], and it's won more awards than any other system in its category[3]. It's commonly acknowledged as having 'changed the game' on dealing with risk[4], and over 150 of the largest investment managers – the people who actually manage your money – use it to assess the risk of over £280 billion in investments.

This book isn't based on my experience then, or on any single person's experience. Instead, it brings together lessons learned over those 20-plus years, based on what works and what doesn't for thousands of financial advisers, who support more than two million people to fund happiness. In other words, **it's based on a unique set of *solid data***.

That solid data is even more crucial with the emergence of AI. I can ask AI almost anything financial in chat format and receive an answer – but it doesn't have the same data sets, nor does it produce the same repeatable, explainable results. It's designed to approximate or guess at what good advice might be, which is fantastic if you want to explore your options and deepen your understanding. But when it comes to taking risk with your life savings, what matters are solid data and tried and tested methods. And that's what this book is based on.

How this book works

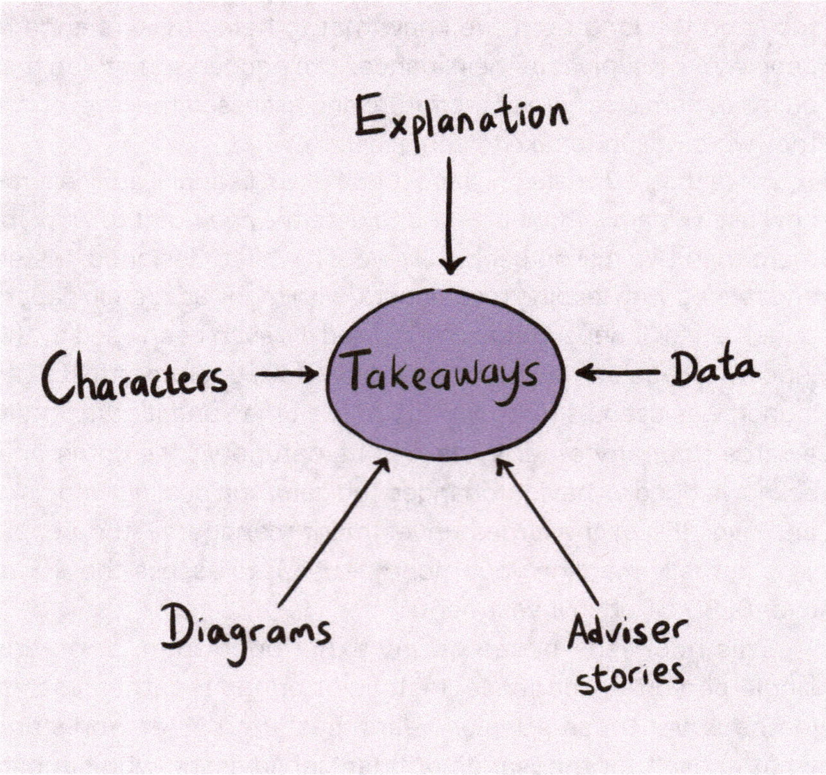

Sound, data-based principles for investing do exist. Our experience at Dynamic Planner has proven that. This book explains those principles in refreshingly clear language, so you don't need to have any financial knowledge to benefit from them.

The explanations are backed up by:

- **Data:** One powerful thing about providing technology that supports financial advice for so many people is the data it produces. Not on individuals, but collectively. That data allows us to see patterns and trends that provide valuable insights for you and your situation. So, throughout the book, we'll use data sourced from Dynamic Planner.
- **Illustrations:** Many people 'don't do numbers', and many of us prefer pictures to words. As well as using data, the book includes simple diagrams to illustrate key concepts.
- **Character journeys:** You'll meet the four characters from the beginning of this chapter again, bringing to life the principles, dilemmas and choices you might face. Sarah, Stephen, Aisha and George aren't real, but they are composites of real-life people encountered by advisers and seen in the data, with very real challenges and opportunities.
- **Adviser stories:** To bridge the gap between principle and practice, I've included snippets from some of the most powerful stories we've heard about the value of financial advice from advisers themselves. All true, but anonymised, they illustrate the benefits of working with an adviser in a way that numbers and diagrams often can't.
- **Takeaways:** To help you keep track of what matters, every chapter ends with a quick summary of its five most important points.

Like any book, you can read this one cover to cover. But if you're in a hurry, you can skim-read the chapters by focusing on the illustrations and the takeaways – or prioritise the chapters that feel relevant to you.

Everything in here is designed for you to discuss with your adviser. Their aim, and the aim of this book, is to help you fund the life you want to live, at a risk that's right for you.

Takeaways

1. Funding happiness means resolving one central dilemma: what truly makes us happy, and how much risk are we willing to take to achieve it?
2. This dilemma is deeply human. Our instincts, shaped over hundreds of thousands of years, lean towards avoiding risk, often leading to short-term comfort but long-term unhappiness.
3. Here's where advisers play a crucial role. A trusted professional can give us the confidence to make choices our instincts might otherwise prevent us from making.
4. This book isn't based on just one person's perspective. Uniquely, it's based on a system refined over more than 20 years, successfully applied by thousands of advisers, to the benefit of more than two million people investing hundreds of billions of pounds between them.
5. Combining data, illustrations and stories, it's designed to help you fund the life you want to live at a risk that's right for you.

1. Funding happiness

Why does happiness need to be funded? While it's true that money alone won't make you happy, try being happy without it.

Think about Sarah, Stephen, Aisha and George. Sarah isn't happy because, in her eyes, she and Stephen are struggling to keep pace with the cost of living. Aisha longs for a secure home to call her own and a garden to play football in with her son, but is unsure how she will afford it. George has money but is worried that it might run out. Lack of money – or perceived lack of money – is a cause of concern for them all.

Money and happiness

Countless philosophers and thinkers have looked at the relationship between money and happiness. More than 2,000 years ago, Aristotle wrote, 'Wealth is evidently not the good we are seeking; for it is *merely useful and for the sake of something else*'[5]. Benjamin Franklin, a philosopher and one of the founders of the United States of America, concluded in the 1700s that 'The *Use of Money* is all the Advantage there is in having Money'[6]. In 2019, when asked whether his wealth had made him happier, Bill Gates said, 'You don't need a billion – but being *free from worry* about financial things is a real blessing'[7].

You get the picture: many have said, in different ways, that money won't buy you happiness, but it is an important tool, a means to an end. For Sarah, Stephen, Aisha and George, as for many of us, money is a source of control: it lets us fund the things we want to do: it lets us fund happiness.

Of course, you don't need to be a philosopher to know that there isn't a direct relationship between happiness and money. Think back to your happiest times; perhaps they involved friends or family sharing a drink, a meal or a laugh together? Or maybe you were taking a quiet walk in nature, listening to a favourite band or watching your team win the league? Together or alone, these things don't necessarily cost very much at all.

But where were you and how did you get there? Almost certainly, you were not hungry or cold, you had clothes you were comfortable in, and you were feeling secure. You may even have been feeling happy in the back of your mind because you had a good career or business, or had had these things in the past, so you were achieving things or expressing yourself in a way that felt good to you. These building blocks for happiness require an exchange or investment of resources, which usually means ... well ... money.

What does money mean to you?

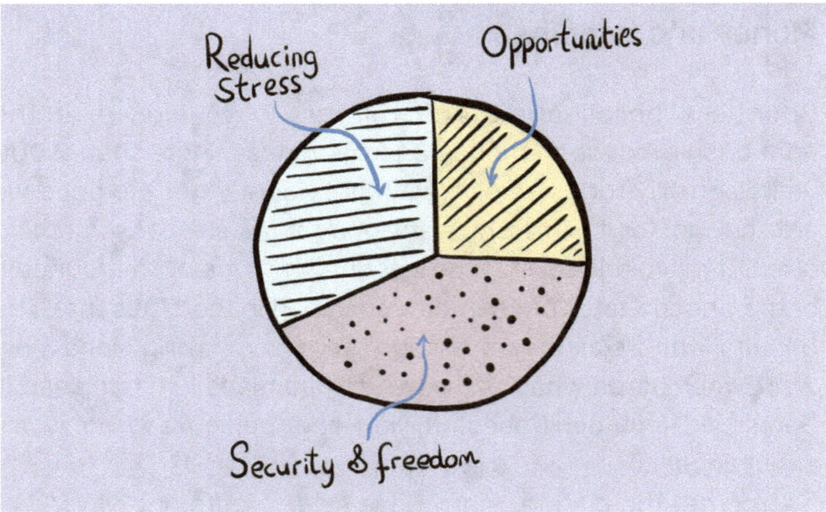

When advisers ask their clients, 'What does money mean to you?', almost half see it as a means of obtaining security and freedom, while close to a third see it as a means of reducing stress. For a quarter, it's a means of providing opportunities. Money, for most of us, is a means to an end[8].

Once we have what we need to get by and are financially secure, the question then becomes, 'What does happiness mean to me?'

Advisers often help their clients think about this by asking what lifestyle changes they would make if money were not a consideration.

For many – like Stephen and George – the dream is to travel and explore; for some, it's having the luxury of time to take things easy or pursue other interests or hobbies. For others, like Aisha, the security of home ownership holds the key to happiness.

If money wasn't a consideration, what would you do or change?

Think about this question your adviser might ask. Here are some of the themes people often come up with – do any of them apply to you, or do you have other dreams or ambitions?

- **Travel and exploration:** Travel more, explore different parts of the world and experience new places. Take regular holidays or bucket-list trips.
- **Retirement or reduced working hours:** Aim for a more balanced lifestyle to allow greater focus on run on leisure and personal interests.
- **Property and lifestyle enhancements:** Improve your lifestyle through hobbies, leisure activities, home renovations or buying larger properties.
- **Financial freedom and spending:** Spend money without constraint, and feel more relaxed about spending on yourself and your family.
- **Philanthropy and social impact:** Help others financially through supporting charities, or engaging in social or charitable work.
- **Health and wellness:** Maintain an active lifestyle, to keep fit and healthy, and reduce stress.

Why do we have to take risk to fund happiness?

To turn your vision of a happy life into reality you will need to take some risks.

Why is that the case? In our working years, as long as we can afford our lifestyle, it's feasible to minimise the level of risk we take with our money, although of course even the safest careers and businesses aren't risk-free. The challenge comes when we want to stop working, achieve financial independence or buy something larger than our income or savings alone can support, such as a house, a car, education for our kids or a new business. Aisha wants both a new home and to set herself up in business, which will require a lot more money than she currently has access to.

While saving is important, when we save into a bank account alone, we're certain to lose money over the long term, because as prices rise over time ('inflation'), the spending power of money falls – a risk in itself. We'll talk more about this later. Unless we're exceptionally well off, we all need a higher return on our money than we can get from a savings account in the bank. Even for the very well off, maintaining wealth requires taking risk, if only to keep pace with inflation. Almost no one is immune.

This is particularly true when it comes to funding retirement: your life after work. In general, we are living longer, and the government and employers are doing less to fund retirement. That means we all have to do more ourselves.

To achieve the kind of returns needed to fund bigger things, and certainly retirement, we need to take risk. Why? Because by taking risk, we put ourselves in a position to earn higher returns. In simple terms, the relationship between risk and return is a little like a seesaw. If you sit close to the centre, the downs are very small and so are the ups, limiting the money you can make ('returns'). The further out on the seesaw you sit, the higher up you can rise: the more money you can make, but also the further you can fall.

The risk seesaw

The risks to your happiness of doing nothing, though – of sitting in the middle of the seesaw – are very real. If your money is not put to good use by taking some level of risk, over time you will almost certainly see a lower standard of living and reduced ability to buy the things that make you and your loved ones happy, because inflation will eat away at the value of your money.

Squaring the circle – taking the level of risk you can afford
The central challenge for people like Sarah and, increasingly, George is that just the idea of taking money out of the bank account and putting it in a position where there is some risk, even in the pursuit of happiness, makes them profoundly unhappy. They feel you are damned if you do and damned if you don't. It is, in short, the Investor's Dilemma.

This book is all about how to resolve the Investor's Dilemma: how far out on the seesaw you need to sit. The life you want, once properly understood and costed, might not actually be as difficult to fund as you imagine.

As the book progresses, you'll see that our characters can in fact resolve their own dilemmas. It may take them a little more time, they may have to spend a bit less, save a bit more or take a bit more risk, but their ideas of happiness are achievable. Time after time, financial advisers tell us that clients can afford to fund their lifestyle or retire far earlier or more easily than they thought if they do two things:

1. Get clear on the things that they want in life. Not the idealised life, but what they *really* want, what *really* makes them happy and what they are prepared to do without to achieve it.

2. Invest enough for the *long term*, taking the right level of risk for them – a level of risk they are willing and able to take for the duration.

What about risks to the planet?

George isn't only concerned about the risks to his money. He's also worried about the future he'll leave for his grandchildren, and therefore about the risks to the planet from his investments. That's the case for more and more of us these days.

How important is investing sustainably?

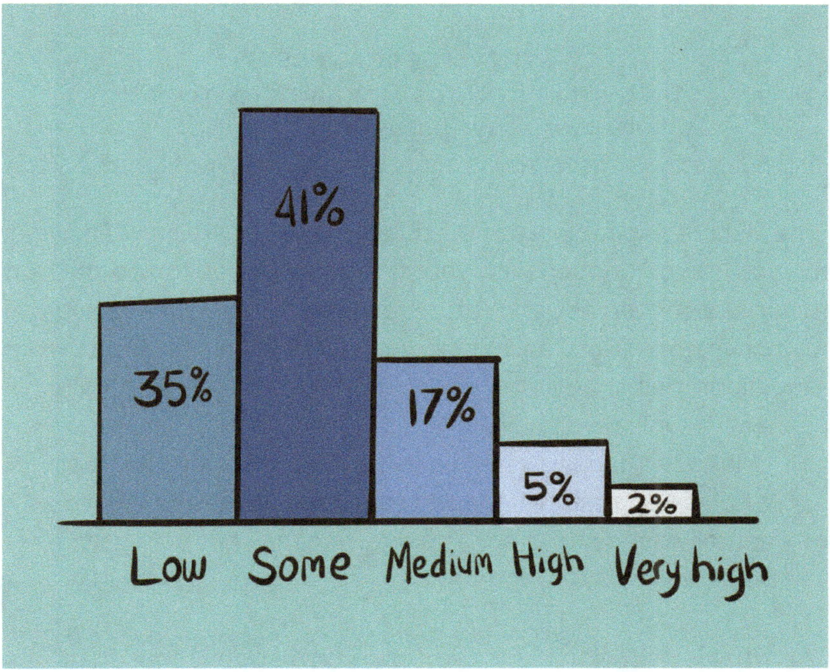

Among more than 40,000 people surveyed in Dynamic Planner, 69% consider the sustainability of their investments to be of 'some importance' to 'very high importance'[9]. Only 35% of people consider it to be of 'low importance'. George is in the largest group and sees sustainability as of 'some importance'. Like most people, he sees what's going on in the world around him. While his principal concerns are financial, he would prefer his investments to do more good than harm.

Historically, investing in a way that's good for the planet as well as good for profits has limited both the pool of investments available and the ability to make money from those investments. Fortunately, today there are a far broader range of investments available to every investor, at every level of risk – from those that simply want to do more good than harm to those who want to make a positive impact with their money.

Resolving the Investor's Dilemma

> **THE VALUE OF ADVICE**
> 'The best thing a client's said to me? "I don't know why I was worrying about money so much."'

The rest of this book looks at the questions to be asked and answered by you, in conjunction with your financial adviser, to find the right balance between risk and future reward – to help you resolve your own Investor's Dilemma. It takes you step-by-step through five key questions, designed to be tackled in sequence:

1. What does happiness mean to you? How do you work out what is important to you and your loved ones and what actually needs funding? The answers may not be what you think.

2. What is risk? Not just in the narrow investment sense but more widely in our financial lives. And how do you find the right level for you?

3. What are the risks to the planet and, by extension, to your money? How can these be better understood so that you can make more informed decisions?

4. How can you successfully resolve the Investor's Dilemma for yourself by building a personal plan and portfolio with your adviser that delivers a balance you are comfortable with?

5. Once you have a plan, how do you build the habits to support it? How do you make the progress you need to fund the life that you want?

Takeaways

1. While money in itself won't bring you happiness, it's an important tool; a means to an end.
2. The funding of a happy life requires taking risk. Doing nothing is, in itself, a risk to your happiness as inflation eats away at the value of your money.
3. The relationship between risk and return is like a seesaw. If you sit close to the centre, the downs are very small but so are the ups. The further out you sit, the more money you can make, but also the further you can fall. You can choose quite precisely where to sit.
4. Most of us want to do more good than harm with our money, and that contributes to our sense of happiness and the planet's health. Today it's far easier to do this and still achieve your financial goals for a level of risk that's right for you.
5. Funding happiness is all about getting the right balance between risk and reward to resolve the Investor's Dilemma.

2. Where a financial adviser will add value . . . and where they won't

We've all been there. Poring over statements and spreadsheets like Stephen and Sarah, scrolling finance apps and chatting with AIs like Aisha, or reading newspapers like George and thinking, 'I could do with some help here. I wish there were someone I could trust to talk to about my finances. Not just the articles I'm reading about different products or best buys or someone else's finances, or what the AI says someone in my situation should consider, but what should *I* do with *my* money.'

There are so many questions:

Am I doing the right thing?
Am I saving enough?
Are we spending too much?
How can I pay less tax?
Can I afford that house?
Are my investments performing well?
Can I afford to retire?
How long will our money last?
Would my loved ones be all right if I died? If I couldn't work?
Am I taking too much risk or being too safe?

These are deeply personal questions, which have their roots in our need to seek security and provide for ourselves and those we care about. As we saw in the last chapter, for many of us, money is about peace of mind.

The challenge is that your personal situation is exactly that: personal to you – or, if you share your finances with a partner, personal to you both. What might work for you might not for your neighbour. The differences depend not only on the financial situation you are in, but on how you feel about money and what you want to do with it. The level of security you're looking for, the level of risk you're willing to take, the life you want to live – in short, what makes you happy.

This is where financial advisers come in. Their role is to help you achieve your goals: to help you build a financial plan or recommend a solution that's right for you. As regulated professionals, they also have the obligation to ensure they understand your situation properly and that they gather enough information to be able to provide you with the best advice they can – advice they can explain to you, and which you can count on.

More than four million people a year take financial advice in the UK, and another 12 million say they would like to benefit from it. Taken together, that's roughly four times the number of people who invest directly and make all the decisions themselves. You are not alone in your desire for help!

Historically, access to quality personal financial advice was restricted because it relied on in-person, face-to-face interaction. The cost of providing it was high, so people who took it typically had more money or valued the benefits more than others.

The good news is that technology is transforming access to personal financial advice from quality financial advisers. Services are increasingly delivered via video call and backed up by the latest app technology, rather than bundles of paper. Today, you can track your financial plan on your mobile, making the whole process far, far easier and more accessible.

The role of an adviser

THE VALUE OF ADVICE

'I met a single mother in her early fifties, a general counsel at a small pharma company. She was worried about funding her retirement and her daughter's education. In our initial call, we discussed her ambitions, concerns and opportunities. After gathering data, my team showed she could retire by her early sixties and fund her daughter's education. To her surprise, she even had enough to retire immediately. This knowledge lifted a burden; she actually chose to work until 68, allowing her daughter to attend Cambridge. Upon retirement, she went on to study history at university herself.'

You should expect your adviser to add value in three ways, which, together, can help you achieve your goals – and improve your peace of mind along the way:

1. As a financial coach
2. With financial planning and tax expertise
3. With investing expertise

We'll look at each of these in turn.

Where advisers add value

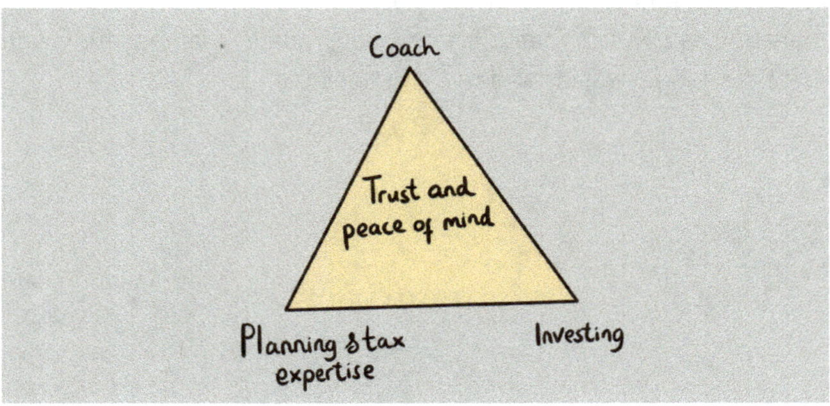

A financial coach

Why do top athletes, successful artists and high-performing executives have coaches and mentors? Because knowing the right thing to do is hard, knowing yourself is even harder, and putting into practice what you know is harder still. Top performers know that working with an objective outsider, someone who can provide external insight, expertise and experience, enhances their self-awareness and helps them go beyond their natural comfort zones.

The same is true for your finances. Understanding your current situation, your approach to money and what will bring you happiness in the future requires time, thought and self-awareness. It requires you to ask yourself the right questions – and to have the objectivity to understand the answers and the discipline to implement them over the long term.

Most of us find it difficult to apply this degree of analysis to our own lives, to see when we are overspending (or, indeed, underspending), to see when we are taking too little risk or too much. And if it's hard in normal times, it's even more so when we're in challenging circumstances, such as after a bereavement, or facing big changes like retirement.

It's also more complicated if you're trying to do it alongside someone else. Stephen and Sarah have quite complicated lives, with a business, two children at university, a mortgage and now Stephen's desire to stop working. They also have quite different ways of thinking about money: Sarah is much more driven by logic and has managed their finances with her spreadsheets over many years. Stephen is driven by emotion. All of this makes it difficult for them to resolve their financial dilemmas together.

A financial adviser has the professional training, methodology, systems and experience to help. If you're planning alone, they're by your side to keep you on track. If you're planning as a couple, they can help you find a common language to talk about what matters, and make sure both parties are heard. That's why a good adviser can be the difference between successfully funding happiness and falling short.

A study conducted by Dynamic Planner with Henley Business School shows people's financial confidence rises when they work with a financial adviser, compared with those who don't[10]. Over time, those who have worked with a financial adviser in the past remain more confident than those who haven't. Trust and peace of mind is built over time – and this positive effect lasts.

Confidence in managing finances

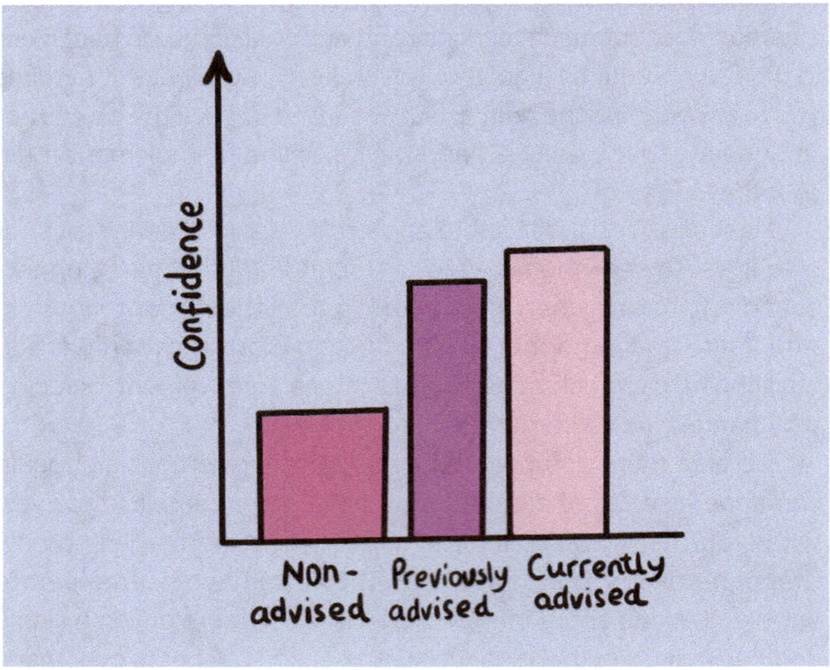

Sarah and Stephen are at a crisis point. They've got a big decision to make, and they've reached an impasse in their efforts to make it themselves. Aisha, too, is on the brink of a life change. After a successful career, and having achieved a comfortable retirement through his own financial research and decision-making, George feels in need of third-party expertise. He needs to avoid running out of money, and the consequences of his investment decisions are beginning to weigh more heavily on him.

It's often moments of truth like these that prompt people to find an adviser. The trigger might be a life event – a change of career, an inheritance, an illness. Or it might be a dawning realisation that the years have slipped by and retirement is looming, or the money might run out.

But if you're not there yet, you don't need to wait. To borrow an old saying about planting a tree: the best time to do it was 20 years ago; the second-best time is now.

Once you start working with a financial adviser, you're underway – and, like a good coach, they can supply the momentum you need to get on track and stay there.

Financial planning and tax expertise

Of course, it's possible to dedicate your time to understanding how to plan your personal finances well, how investments work, how to minimise tax and how to structure investments so that you don't take unnecessary risks. But most of us also have our own work to do, a home to look after, and perhaps kids or older relatives to care for.

For a financial adviser, staying on top of all this is their job. They take exams and are required to keep learning throughout their careers to ensure they understand the issues that can affect your finances. They follow structured, regulated processes to give you the best chance of achieving the financial outcomes you are looking for.

For well over a decade the financial advice profession has developed better and better ways of helping their clients, both in theory and in practice[11]. Many firms also hold Chartered Insurance Institute (CII) chartered status, which recognises a high level of technical competence, as well as adherence to a code of ethics.

Financial planning is a constantly changing field, in which keeping up with the latest developments can often save you money through tax efficiencies or better fee structures. So for anyone other than a real enthusiast, it makes sense to lean on a financial adviser's expertise.

Investing

There's very little evidence that DIY investors are able to beat the professionals or even match them, and there's a lot of evidence to show they are almost always their own worst enemy.

A famous study on this topic was conducted in the US by Barber and Odean[12]. These two professors found that, in summary, 'trading is hazardous to your wealth'. A series of handicaps such as lack of knowledge, behavioural biases and overconfidence tend to lead private investors to do worse from their own investment choices than they would have by simply tracking the market[13].

Independent research firm Dalbar found the same in a study of the performance of the average investor, again in the US, since 1984[14]. $100,000 invested by the average equity investor in the US 30 years ago would now be worth just over $1 million. But if they'd simply invested it and left it to track a basket of shares representing the average of all companies, it would be worth over $1.8 million. Dalbar's research consistently shows that individual investors get it wrong by trying to predict the timing of market rises and falls, piling into stocks that are already doing well, or selling investments when their value is down to avoid further losses.

In other words, getting the returns you need by yourself is hard. As a professional, your financial adviser will have access to training, systems and resources that put them in a good position to help you achieve a better outcome than you would on your own.

That's not to say they will be an expert stock picker – the days of personal stockbrokers making tips and trades are well and truly behind us. Instead, financial advisers are concerned with getting you the best long-term returns you can achieve, based on the right level of risk for you and your preferences for important issues such as environmental sustainability.

Dalbar study: Performance of the average investor compared to the market ($100,000 invested over 30 years)

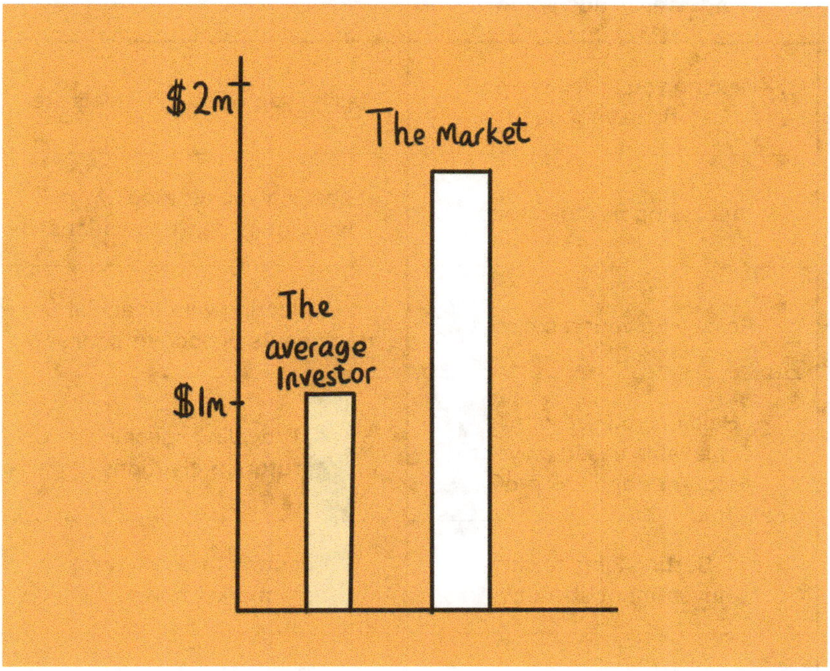

Getting the most from the relationship

We've covered where you can expect your adviser to add value. What about where you should not expect them to? There are some common misunderstandings about what the role of a good adviser actually is — and to get the most from the relationship, there are things you need to do yourself.

The better you understand the division of responsibility, and the more you engage with what your adviser needs from you, the more you'll get from the relationship.

Where you can expect your adviser to add value	**... and where they won't**
Helping you articulate and prioritise your goals	Telling you what your goals are
Assessing risk tolerance	Labelling you as 'medium' risk without in-depth questions
Reviewing your resources	Collecting your financial documents or accounts for you
Helping you see what's achievable based on your resources and risk profile	Providing specific future projections
Setting long-term investment strategy	Reacting to short-term market news
Minimising tax on investments	Completing your tax return (though they might recommend an accountant)
Identifying risks to your life plan and recommending appropriate insurance	Researching home and car insurance for you
Encouraging you to stay invested, in bad markets as well as good	Trading you in and out of the market
Rebalancing your investment over time based on long-term needs or performance	Pushing the latest investment idea or 'hot stock'
Monitoring your progress against your plan	Controlling your saving and spending habits

Frequent concerns about using an adviser

THE VALUE OF ADVICE
'The best compliment is those who initially feel that they don't want ongoing advice and then come back to us and sign up for our ongoing service a year or two down the line.'

Aisha has been thinking about getting some advice for months, but never quite got around to it. Her situation is very common: in fact, in a given year, almost three times as many people say they want to get financial advice as actually take it.

What gets in the way? As well as our busy lives and long to-do lists, there are some common concerns and preconceptions many of us share that prevent us from accessing the help and advice we need. Many of these are hangovers from the past, before the industry was regulated in the way it is today.

Let's look at some of those concerns, versus the realities of receiving advice.

'I'll have to pay'

Yes, your adviser will charge you – in fact, wouldn't it be strange if they didn't? If you're looking for help with your finances, you want to work with an objective professional who can afford to invest in the qualifications, training and infrastructure they need to support you. That's worth paying for, just like you'd pay a solicitor, an accountant or any other skilled professional.

There's also plenty of research to show that financial advice pays for itself. A study by investment group Vanguard found working with an adviser who uses recommended industry best practices increases the average return by about three percentage points – which means if you'd achieved a 4% return on your own, working with an adviser could have got you 7%[15]. Another study from advice giant Quilter, bringing together the findings of more than 40 academic papers, puts the average impact at 3% or more a year[16].

Advice fees do come on top of the fees you pay for the financial products you invest in. But advice firms have structured processes for assessing the value of financial products, and they will negotiate on your behalf. That means it's not uncommon for the total fees paid by advised clients to be the same or even lower than those paid by people using DIY investment platforms.

'They're biased'

At the start of this century, this concern might well have been justified. Advisers were paid through commission, which may have incentivised them to recommend certain products over others – and there was no requirement for them to look beyond those products. However, in 2013 the UK's financial regulator, the FCA, banned commissions. Now, the adviser gets paid the same regardless of the investment products they recommend, and is instead paid fees just like any other professional (another reason why paying for advice is positive!).

Commission payments still exist for products like mortgages and life insurance, but there are much more stringent obligations on financial advisers and the companies they work for to make sure their recommendations are suitable for you. And whatever they're helping you with, advisers have to be transparent about the range of products and product providers they cover, as well as how they get paid.

'They just want to sell me things'

Again, prior to 2013, this might have been true. When advisers were paid through commission on investments, they were motivated to sell as many products as possible.

There are various ways to pay for advice today, but the typical model is to pay an annual charge – either a percentage of your assets or a set fee – that covers all the advice you receive, whether that's related to investment funds, retirement planning or insurance and protection.

The more assets you have, the more responsibility an adviser is taking on and also the greater their ability to add value to your investments. As a result, you will pay more in absolute terms for larger amounts invested. However, most firms offer tiered fees, with the percentage charge reducing as portfolio size increases, recognising that costs don't rise in proportion.

If you don't want the full service, firms typically also offer a menu of services with set fees for one-off pieces of advice, so you can pick and choose what you need and pay accordingly. A small but increasing number of firms provide a subscription service, where you can pay for advice on an affordable monthly basis.

Whatever their charging model, almost all firms offer a free initial consultation so they can get an overview of your situation and what you want to achieve, and so you can assess whether you'd like to work with them.

'I'll feel vulnerable'

This is a concern for many people who haven't worked with a financial adviser before. What we do with our money is personal, and many of us were raised not to discuss it at all. Some, like George, have managed their finances for decades on their own without anyone else involved. It's no surprise, then, that the idea of talking to an adviser might create a certain feeling of vulnerability. There are few of us who don't feel embarrassed or concerned about some aspect of how we manage our money, whether that's not saving enough, spending too much or not getting round to thinking about it at all. But experienced advisers have these conversations every day, so they're used to putting people at ease, and you won't say anything they haven't heard before.

That first conversation might feel awkward, but finding someone you trust to help you make important decisions for your future can be a huge relief. Of course, you need to feel comfortable, so if you're searching for a financial adviser, it's good practice to have initial conversations with at least three to find a good fit.

'I haven't got the time'

To get good financial advice, you need to speak to an adviser, and they need to speak to you. You both need time to build trust. Traditionally this is achieved face-to-face – and you might still find that approach more comfortable. But with the greater availability of technology such as video calls and mobile apps, financial advisers and their advice are much more accessible than they were even a few years ago, and can fit more easily into a busy life.

How you speak to your adviser is a matter of personal choice. An in-person meeting can often be the first interaction to help build the relationship, but then subsequent meetings might be by video. Increasing numbers of companies offer video or phone-based advice only. Whatever the approach, even the most traditional firms will provide you with online interaction so the process of data gathering, getting to know you and reporting to you takes up much less of your time.

'It's all or nothing'

Working with an adviser doesn't have to be all or nothing – complete delegation or complete DIY. There are a range of approaches, and you can choose the one that's right for you.

Some of the most common are:

- **Transactional support:** The adviser provides specific help with a specific question or product, for a set fee.

- **Fee-based planning:** The adviser works with you to build a long-term financial plan, as a one-off or with an annual progress review.

- **Investment and wealth management**: The adviser manages your money over the long term, based on your risk profile and financial plan.

Aisha, for example, might be better off just getting a one-off piece of advice about a mortgage and putting enough aside to afford the deposit and set herself up as a freelancer. Stephen and Sarah's situation is considerably more complex, so they might want to choose a fee-based financial plan to look at different scenarios. Meanwhile, George's concerns about continuing to manage his pensions and investments might mean a wealth management service is more appropriate. It's not one-size-fits-all.

Takeaways

1. The adviser's role is to work with you to create a tailored plan or set of financial solutions aligned to your goals, risk profile and preferences, which supports your long-term financial security and happiness.
2. A good adviser will act as a coach, providing objectivity, professional insight and motivation – especially valuable during life's transitions and market ups and downs.
3. You can rely on your adviser to stay up to date on tax and investment planning complexities. While they're not accountants, they will look to save you money.
4. Studies show DIY investors often lose out on returns. Your adviser won't send you the latest stock tips, but they will work with you to set a strategy to meet your goals and help you get the best returns over the long term, for the risk you're willing and able to take.
5. Depending on your adviser's firm, they might offer a range of services, digital and/or in person, from holistic financial planning and advice to more transactional support with specific products, depending on your needs.

3. What is happiness?

> 'Would you tell me, please, which way I ought to go from here?' said Alice.
> 'That depends a good deal on where you want to get to,' said the Cat.
> 'I don't much care where–' said Alice.
> 'Then it doesn't matter which way you go,' said the Cat.
>
> *Alice's Adventures in Wonderland,* Lewis Carroll

For each of our four characters, happiness means something different. It's shaped by their own experiences, values and, importantly, their stage of life. For Stephen, happiness increasingly lies in freedom and fulfilment beyond work. After years of building his graphic design business, he dreams of travelling and reconnecting with places where he and Sarah spent time volunteering when they first met. Happiness for Stephen is a chance to rediscover his purpose, and experience life outside business commitments again.

For Sarah, happiness feels much more grounded in the security of the family's current life and shared responsibilities. A maths teacher with a practical, logical outlook, she values stability and a secure future, certainly over the next few years while their two children are still in education. While Stephen's vision isn't unattractive, Sarah's happiness stems from knowing their financial foundation is strong and they're able to support their commitments together. It's Sarah who runs the household's finances, and getting the numbers to add up on her spreadsheet is a source of real comfort to her.

Aisha finds happiness in spending time with her son. Her dream is a house with a garden for him to play in. Balancing work and motherhood, she sees freelancing as a way to secure her financial independence while being more present. Happiness for Aisha is being around more for her son and watching him grow up while knowing they will both be financially secure.

For George, the retired GP, happiness is rooted in memories and connections. His family home, trips to visit his daughter in Australia and quiet time in his garden represent a life well lived, both past and present. He has an active social circle and enjoys golf as well as his travel. Happiness for him now means ensuring his finances can continue to support him for many years to come, and hopefully leaving something to his daughter and grandchildren once he's gone.

The more clearly our characters can identify what brings them happiness, the better placed they are to make the right decisions about their money. The same is true for you. The key to turning your money into a tool for your own happiness is to understand what you want it to do for you. To be clear about where you want to go so that it's easier to get there. Exploring your version of happiness is the first step to designing a financial plan that's not just financially sound but also really satisfying.

Why is happiness important?

THE VALUE OF ADVICE

'Relationships improve when you understand a client's purpose, their values and drivers. How they make difficult decisions, what annoys them and what makes them happy. Who they want to be.'

Happiness isn't a big topic in the financial press, nor is it part of any financial education at school, but what are you working and putting away money for, if not for your happiness and that of those you care about?

In your first conversation with your adviser, it's likely they will ask you a question along the lines of 'What are you looking to achieve?' or 'What are your goals?'.

These apparently simple questions can actually be very hard to answer, not least because we know that most people – and perhaps this is true for you – don't have specific goals or objectives.

This word cloud summarises the responses from 30,000 adviser clients to the question 'What are your objectives?', with the larger words showing the most popular responses[17].

As you can see, 'investment', 'income', 'growth', 'pension' and 'retirement' are the most popular. But is this really what will make the respondents happy? Is it really, to quote Lewis Carroll's rabbit, 'where you want to get to'? Surely 'investment' is a means to an end, as is 'retirement'?

Stephen wants to volunteer and travel, Sarah wants security, Aisha wants to spend more time with her son, George wants peace of mind… and so on. Over the last ten years, the financial services industry has transformed from one that was mostly product-centric (pensions, investments, funds etc) to one that's increasingly customer-centric, i.e., all about you. What do you want?

Responses to the question 'What are your objectives?'

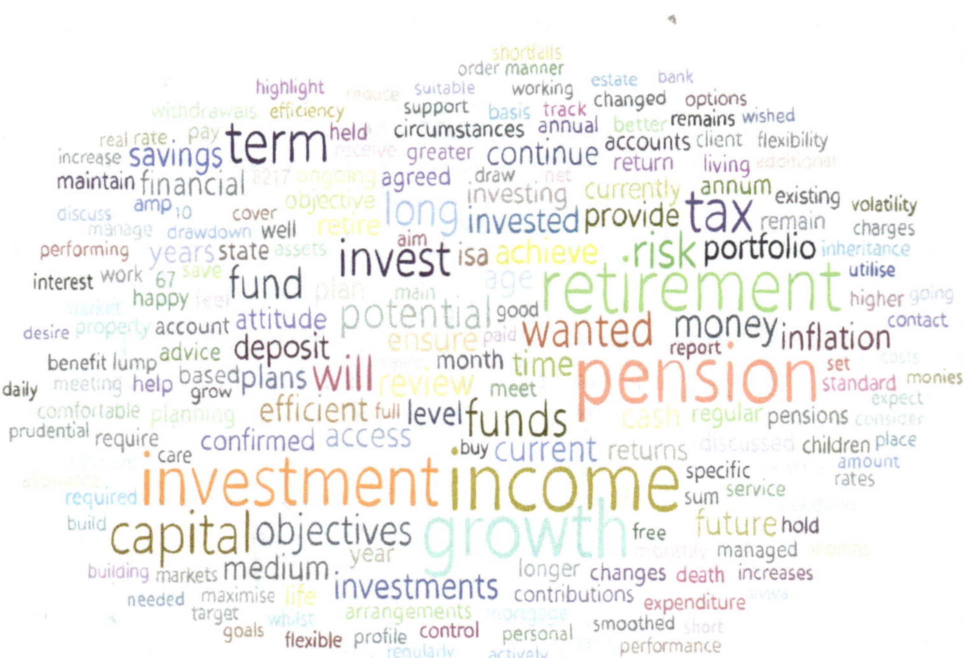

The ideal future

Our latest research tries to get beyond the product-based answers to the heart of what people really want, through more probing questions such as 'What would your ideal future look like?' These responses are much more meaningful – here are some that come up most often:

- **Comfortable retirement:** A very common vision includes a financially secure retirement with the ability to travel and enjoy life without financial stress.
- **Maintaining living standards:** Many aim to keep being able to afford the things they can now, or improve on their current living standards.
- **Family wellbeing:** Ensuring the financial stability and wellbeing of family members is a priority for lots of people.

Modern financial planning, as you will see in the following chapters, is all about helping you to pay for the things that are important to you, while taking the amount of risk that's right for you. Being as clear as you can about what makes you happy and having those conversations with your adviser provides you with your 'why': a 'true north' based on which to build your plans.

Why is understanding the relationship between money and happiness so difficult?

> **THE VALUE OF ADVICE**
>
> 'A client doubled his salary moving to a new firm, so I asked, "Are you an £80k person now or still a £40k person?" He replied, "I'm still a £40k person, I'm happy." I suggested he "pretend" he was still earning £40k and save the difference, which built him a nice pot. Years later, he doubled his salary again. This time, when I asked, he laughed, "I know what you're going to say! But yes, I've become an £80k person – and now an £80k person wants to spend like a £160k person."'

The relationship between your money and your happiness is likely to change throughout your life. Academic research in the US historically suggested a direct relationship between money and happiness – but one that persisted only up to a point. Happiness increased as incomes did, up to around $75,000 a year, but then it levelled off even as income rose[18]. The assumption was therefore that money had less of a happiness effect once a certain level of needs were met. However, more recent work suggests that for most people larger incomes are actually associated with greater happiness, with no levelling off. The exception is people who are financially well off but unhappy. 'If you are rich and miserable, more money won't help'[19].

As our incomes and wealth rise, often the cost of what we want rises too. Similarly, as incomes in retirement fall, so can expenditure – and people are often surprised to find they're content with less. Key to funding happiness will be working out how to ensure your money and your goals are in balance. Your adviser won't be able to tell you what your goals are, but they will be able to ask the right questions to help you think about them, prioritise them and achieve that balance.

'Needs' versus 'wants'

Money can help us get what we need. Beyond that, it can help us achieve what we want, and even what we dream of. This is a useful division when you're thinking about your future.

What do you need – what are your 'must haves'? How much money will it take to cover your basic costs and feel safe?

What do you want? What would you 'like to have'? And what's the role of money in achieving what you dream of? We'll work through this together later in the book.

Scarcity versus abundance

As well as our express needs and wants, our attitudes toward money are shaped, in part, by our environment, as well as by our parents and their parents before them.

For example, academic research found 'people in the most deprived areas were more likely to prefer smaller-sooner rewards than people from the least deprived areas. Similarly, people in technical or routine occupations tended to prefer smaller-sooner rewards than people in professional or intermediate occupations'[20].

If a parent lost a job or their business failed when you were a child, that shock to the family's finances can run deep. If you're close to retirement today and you grew up in the UK or Europe, you might also be carrying around values forged in the extreme austerity of the interwar and postwar years when your parents' parents grew up and formed their own values.

If you were raised with a scarcity mindset, you may have learned to see money, work and other resources as fundamentally limited. You might struggle to spend even when you can afford to do so. The idea of taking any kind of risk with your money can feel frightening. Sarah's experience of family precarity as a child deeply colours her view of money today and the importance to her of managing everything carefully.

Perhaps the attitudes that have been handed down to you are serving you well. Or perhaps, when you notice them, you might find they're holding you back. Maybe you find it hard to increase your earnings because you don't believe the work opportunities are out there, for example – or because you fear jeopardising what you have now by reaching for a higher-paid role or bigger business opportunity. The stories we tell ourselves about money can be self-fulfilling. If that's the case, the exercises in this book will be extra important as they can help you get beyond those tightly held beliefs to what really matters to you.

The impact of risk on happiness

When it comes to risk-taking, we're not only dealing with the legacy of our parents and grandparents but our entire inheritance as humans. For a long time, economists had assumed we acted 'rationally' when it came to risk and reward: we would carefully weigh up the costs and benefits, and if it was more likely that we'd make money, as opposed to losing it, we would be willing to take the risk.

However, psychologists Daniel Kahneman and Amos Tversky found that was not the case. They devised a powerful experiment in which participants were asked if they would take a bet based on the outcome of a coin toss, heads or tails.

For example, they were asked if they would take a bet where:

Heads: You lose $100
Tails: You win $150

If humans were rational, we'd take that bet. But it turns out most people wouldn't take the bet until the amount they might win is *more than twice* what they might lose[21]. In other words, the prospect of a loss can cause more than twice as much pain as the pleasure that results from the prospect of an equivalent gain.

Kahneman and Tversky's work showed that people experience losses more intensely than gains. This loss aversion means the chances are that, consciously or subconsciously, your brain may be discouraging you from acting in your own best interests when it comes to your finances.

The risk of loss is difficult for the great majority of people, but it's harder for some people than others – again, think back to Sarah and Stephen. Understanding your own feelings about risk is central to funding happiness – and a big part of what an adviser can help you with. If you're not taking enough risk, you won't achieve the gains you need to fund your goals. On the other hand, if you're taking too much risk for your own comfort, the worry along the way may outweigh the pleasure you get from the gains you ultimately achieve. Most concerningly, if this applies to you, you're less likely to stay the course. We'll look more at how to get the balance right later.

What's holding you back?

As we've discussed, money is a means to an end – something you can make use of to achieve comfort and happiness. But sometimes it can feel like something's getting in the way. If that applies to you, here are some things you can do.

Check your habits

Some of us, like Sarah, balance our budgets every week, while some go months without looking at their bank account. Some people are only happy if they know where every last penny is; some are more broad-brush. Some of us have budget spreadsheets or different pots for different purposes. Some buy on impulse, some shop around for a deal. Some set rules – only one takeaway a month – and stick to them, some don't stick to them, and some don't set them in the first place.

These habits matter because, over time, they can roll up to big amounts. 'We are what we repeatedly do' is a summary of Aristotle's view of the importance of habits[22]. That might be great news. If you already set a budget and keep to it, putting some aside to save, those savings can mount up. Equally, if you overspend a little every month, so too can the debts start to build. We'll look more at budgeting and habits in chapter 13. For now, it's worth noting that getting your short-term finances in balance is a stepping stone to longer-term happiness.

Debt: Friend or foe?

Some people think all debt is bad: 'neither a borrower nor a lender be'. Many religions prohibited debt historically, and some still do. Other people have fallen into the trap of taking on more and more debt – a sure-fire path to unhappiness. Some people use debt as a tool and manage it well, taking on debts to fund investments that otherwise would have been impossible for them – buying their own home or funding a business, like Aisha wants to, for example.

In the UK, 83% of adults hold at least one credit or loan product, so the use of debt is something most of us have to learn to manage well[23]. If you're one of the 30% or so of people who have a mortgage[24], it's very likely to be your biggest debt. On average, your monthly payment is likely to cost more than a fifth of your household income. For those like Aisha who are just getting on the property ladder, it can be a third or more.

Once the mortgage is paid off, many people, like George, report a huge sense of freedom. Owning your own home is a dream that resonates in many countries around the world – and owning it outright can bring significant psychological comfort.

The role of debt in your life and your financial plan isn't straightforward then. We'll explore it in more detail later.

Cake now or cake later?

Stephen's impulsivity means he often prioritises short-term gratification like a nicer holiday or eating out over long-term financial stability. Managing impulsivity really matters when it comes to your long-term finances, but it's not always easy to do.

You might have heard of the Marshmallow Test, developed at Stanford University in the 1970s. To evaluate their ability to delay gratification, children were given a marshmallow and told they could eat it immediately—or they could wait 15 minutes and get to keep the first marshmallow and be given a second one. Even at a young age, some kids were much better than others at postponing the treat for a larger reward later. Subsequent research—including a recent rerun—found all sorts of reasons why that might be the case, from socioeconomic status to family background and biology[25].

If you recognise yourself as the kid who lunges for the marshmallow, building and sticking to a longer-term financial plan might be harder, but is all the more important. If you're thoughtful about how you design your financial life, you can make it easier to do the right thing and harder to do things that don't support your long-term happiness—again, your adviser can help.

Takeaways

1. Happiness was rarely discussed in financial planning in the past, but to set meaningful goals, it's essential to understand what makes you happy.
2. Everyone's vision of happiness is unique, whether it involves living modestly or enjoying luxury. Identifying what truly brings you joy will make it easier than you think to fund happiness.
3. Distinguishing between needs and wants is a useful way to start formulating your goals.
4. Humans aren't rational about taking risk—it's in our nature to be cautious. But without risk our goals are likely to remain out of reach. It's all about finding a balance.
5. Developing good habits, delaying gratification and aligning your spending with your goals can significantly enhance financial security and your happiness.

4. What does happiness mean to you?

As we've seen, our four characters all have their own versions of happiness. And you'll have yours.

It is useful to spend some time thinking about your vision of happiness before you sit down with your adviser to start making a financial plan. Your adviser can help you think through your needs, but they can't tell you what will make you happy, any more than they can tell you what your favourite colour is.

The three exercises in this chapter are designed to help you take that step.

You can just do the first one, or you can work through them all, depending how much time you want to spend on the process and how deep you want to go.

Some tips for success:

- **Set aside time:** Work through these exercises when you have the time and space to think about them. Find somewhere quiet, away from your work, where you can let your mind relax. Even better, take a morning or even a weekend or holiday to remove yourself from your day-to-day pressures and give yourself some perspective. If you get stuck, try thinking about them while taking a walk in a park or the countryside.

- **Grab a pen or laptop:** Rather than trying to balance your priorities in your head, write them down. Writing about your goals makes them real and tangible. The more visual, the better – then you can look at what you've written and refine it.

- **Go solo, then together:** If you're planning with a partner, try to do the exercises separately and only then look at them together. A good shared vision of happiness is more likely to emerge when both partners give themselves the freedom to explore their individual visions *first*.

Quick and easy: must do / like to / dream of

THE VALUE OF ADVICE

'One couple's goal was to own a second property in New Zealand, where one of them had family. But when they discussed what was important, they realised being able to spend more time with their children over here mattered more to them. They actually reduced their working hours, rather than continuing to work hard to achieve a goal they now understood was a "nice to have", not a necessity.'

The first exercise is the Dynamic Planner way. It begins with a simple budgeting exercise and becomes a powerful approach to thinking about where you are now and where you want to get to. You'll need your bank, investment and credit card or loan statements for the past three months. Or, if you already have a budgeting app or spreadsheet, you can use that instead.

Looking at where your money goes over a three-month period should give you a good sense of both regular outgoings (direct debits and standing orders) and also other types of spending, planned and unplanned. Depending on the period you've chosen, you might also need to factor in 'high days and holidays': Christmas, birthdays, travel and other events that fall outside the ordinary. These 'exceptions', as well as household emergencies such as a broken washing machine or a problem with the car, happen more often than we think. Forgetting them is often where people's financial plans fall down.

What are you paying now?

Using the first table in Appendix 1, start by looking at what you're spending money on now:

- Which of these costs are for essentials – things you *must* do?
- Which are for things you *like* to do?
- Which of your costs, if any, are to achieve the things you *dream* of?

Before we move on to thinking about the future, this is a good opportunity to notice any spending patterns that aren't making you happy, or things you'd like to change. Do you really need or want all of those subscriptions? Could the mortgage, energy, mobile or streaming bills be reduced by shopping around?

Your list is also a useful foundation for keeping track of your spending. Developing the habit of revisiting it from time to time is good housekeeping for your happiness.

What do you want the future to look like?

Once you've completed the 'now' column, it's time to think about the future. Put the table with your current spending to one side and think openly and creatively about what you want from your life in the future. Some people find it helps to doodle; others prefer to build lists in a spreadsheet or notepad – or now might be a good time for that walk.

At this stage, don't worry about whether or how this future life can be funded. Think about what would make you happy, trying to make the pictures as rich and detailed as possible. If you want to travel: how often, where to and how? Do you like roughing it, camping or driving a motorhome? Or is your dream holiday in a beautiful villa, a five-star hotel or perhaps a holiday place of your own?

The next step is to make your creative thinking more concrete, bringing your desired future life into focus and reality. Whether you've got notes, sketches or ideas, pull them into a list and try to add timeframes, or life phases for each thing to happen – it doesn't matter if these are rough. Table 2 in Appendix 1 can help.

If you're making plans as a couple, share what you've come up with, perhaps over a meal or a glass of wine. How similar are they? Where are they different?

For inspiration, let's look at how some of our characters tackled this exercise.

Aisha's life phases

My life phases : Aisha	
What?	When?
Senior Project Manager	Now
Buy first home	Next 12 months?
Go freelance	In next 2 years
Sammy goes to uni	12 years' time
Travel more?	15 years' time
Retirement	68

Aisha is currently 35. She knows she wants to go freelance to spend more time with her son, and she also wants to buy her first home. In the longer term, maybe when Sammy's at university, she would like to set up her own consultancy business. This exercise helps her to identify some timeframes and prioritise her goals. While the life phases she identifies are broad brush sketches, they begin to paint a helpful picture.

Stephen and Sarah's life phases

My life phases Stephen & Sarah		
What	When/Age	
Both Working	Stephen 56	Sarah 51
Stephen part time/more travel	60	55
Stephen retires/charity work	67	62
Sarah retires	67	62
Travel/Charity work together	67	62
Later retirement	80+	80+

As we know, Stephen, who's 56, wants to stop working as soon as possible and focus on charity work – something he and Sarah did when they first met. On reflection and when he and Sarah talk calmly through this exercise, he can envisage working as he is now until he's 60 and then perhaps working part time in his business for a while.

Sarah is a little younger, at 51. Her work as a teacher and now head of year is tiring but she loves it! She wants to keep doing it for at least the next ten years. Beyond that, she'd love them both to stop working completely and recapture the adventurous spirit of their youth by fulfilling a long-held dream of hers: travelling around Europe together in a camper van. Spending time with their children and, she hopes, grandchildren is another important priority for her. Before retiring, Sarah would like to travel more with Stephen in the school holidays – in fact, maybe that camper van dream could start now?

Stephen and Sarah want slightly different things from their later years, but it's a good start that they're able to sketch out the basic life phases as they see them. Although Stephen's desire for a change was the trigger for them to start planning for the future, doing the exercise separately first has given Sarah an opportunity to focus on her own goals, which are now less likely to get lost and cause resentments between the couple later.

George's life phases

My life phases: George	
What?	When/Age
Active retirement	75
Golf, tennis, travel	75 As long as I can
Downsize	85?
Take things a bit easier?	85+
Health care?	85+
Legacy gifts?	85+

George is still healthy and active at 75. The loss of his wife and some of his friends has made him very aware of the uncertainty of the future at this stage of life, but he's keen to make the most of his hobbies and trips to Australia for as long as he can. He enjoys his life in retirement and has deep roots in his community, but the large family house and garden are becoming more difficult to look after. This exercise helps him put a possible timeframe on his vague thoughts about downsizing and focus on what he might be able to leave his daughter by way of a legacy. As a retired GP who's also been into hospital recently for a minor operation, he's also aware of the need to factor in the costs of healthcare as he ages.

How long to plan for

You'll notice none of the characters have set an end date for their plans. That's fine – they're all in good health. That said, it's increasingly seen as good practice to plan your finances until at least age 90 and even age 100. Using simple averages, a woman who is 35 today, like Aisha, can still expect to be alive at 90. More than three quarters of women her age are expected to be alive at 80; more than half are expected to live to over 90, and 10% are expected to make it to 100. Aisha should therefore plan to make sure her money can support her until she's at least 90.

Life expectancy for those born in 1990

Age (Years)	% of Men Alive	% of Women Alive
40	97%	98%
50	95%	97%
60	91%	94%
70	84%	89%
80	69%	78%
90	39%	52%
100	5%	10%

Percentage of population born in 1990 expected to survive to each age, based on mid-level expectations of future mortality improvements.

This is data for the UK, where people are generally living longer than in the past. Although it is slowing again now, life expectancy has grown by approximately two years every decade due to improvements in healthcare, medical technology and living conditions, as well as growing awareness of the impact of a healthy lifestyle.

While none of us can know how long we'll live, our plans should reflect our increasing longevity and the need to manage our resources accordingly. For many of us, that will involve a radical shift away from the traditional model of education, followed by a career and family, followed by retirement.

In their excellent book *The 100-Year Life,* Lynda Gratton and Andrew Scott talk about how much has changed for people today, not just in the increasing health and longevity that we're statistically more likely to enjoy, but in the nature of work itself. Jobs for life like George's are increasingly rare, but as certainty of employment has fallen, the opportunities available to create income and build wealth have grown[26]. Your life phases might include multiple careers – something to think about as you're drawing up your vision of happiness.

Your life might include several phases

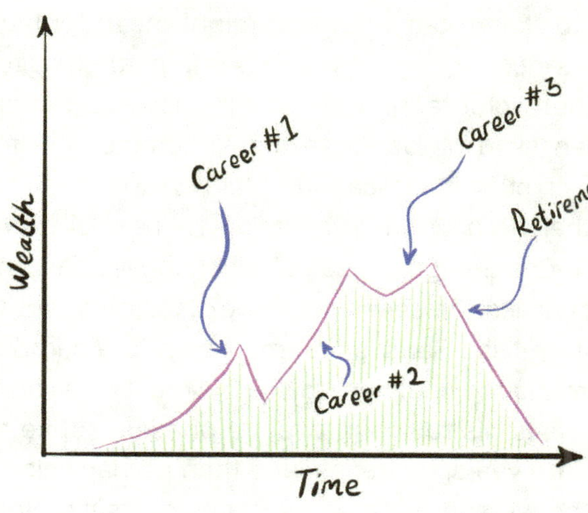

Of course, life rarely unfolds exactly as planned. The potential impact of life events such as accidents, illness and divorce, as well as redundancy and business issues, will eventually need to be factored into your plan to ensure you're as well prepared as you can be. We'll come to that later.

How much might all this cost?

You've turned your hopes and dreams for the future into something more tangible. Now, use table 3 in Appendix 1 to see how your income and expenses might change in the different phases you've sketched out.

Aisha expects her income to be relatively stable in the short term while she's staying put in her job in order to buy a home. She's done some research into the mortgages she could get and the houses she could afford, and she expects to pay out a little less each month on housing once she owns a place.

Her priority when she goes freelance isn't to earn more but to make similar money while working fewer hours, with more flexibility. At that point, her commuting costs will come down and she won't need so much childcare either, so they might be able to afford more holidays. Her opportunity for a higher income comes when Sammy goes off to university and she starts her consulting business. She starts to sketch out what that might mean for her finances.

Stephen's income will fall as he moves from full-time to part-time work and then volunteering for charity. However, he can expect certain expenses to fall too – for example, commuting into the office or eating lunch out with colleagues. Stephen and Sarah like to travel abroad for their holidays each year and have been all over the world. They love Europe though, and as Stephen moves part time, they're happy to spend less on seeing far-flung places. Instead, they agree they'd like to realise Sarah's dream of buying a camper van and travelling around the continent to see the great cities and beaches.

George sees his future in two life phases: active retirement for another ten years, he hopes, and then perhaps slowing down, selling the house and making fewer trips overseas. Because he's

Aisha life phases

Life Phase	Senior project manager	Freelance	Consultant
Dates	From... To...	From... To...	From... To...
Incomes			
Monthly income (after tax)	£4,000	£4,000	£9,000
Expenses			
Rent / mortgage	£1,400	£1,200	£1,200
Childcare	£500	£200	£0
Commuting	£500	£0	£0
Household expenses	£1,500	£1,500	£1,000
Holidays and travel	£2,500 annually	£3,500 annually	£5,000 annually

Stephen and Sarah life phases

Life Phase	Full time	Part time	Charity
Dates	From... To...	From... To...	From... To...
Incomes			
Monthly income (after tax)	£10,000	£5,000	£0
Expenses			
Commuting	£1,000	£250	£0
Eating lunch out	£200	£100	£0
Holidays	£5,000 annually	£2,500 annually	£2,500 annually

aware that he might need to spend more on medical care in the second phase, he does a bit of research online to check what someone coming in to assist him might cost.

George life phases

Life Phase	Active retirement	Later retirement
Dates	From... To...	From... To...
Incomes		
Monthly income (after tax)	£7,000	£7,000
Expenses		
Everyday expenses	£4,000 a month	£4,000 a Month
House maintenance	£200	£100
Annual trip to Australia	£10,000 annually	£0
Other travel	£10,000 annually	£0
Medical costs	£0	£4,000 a month

You get the picture. To start this exercise, you don't need to be too precise about what future incomes and expenses might be. However, the more detail you can add the more you can flesh out the future you want. Beginning with your incomes and expenses today provides you with a realistic starting point so you can think about how you want things to change.

We've already seen that that prices tend to rise over time, and that's also true of incomes. However, don't worry about that when you're setting out your table – your adviser can help you factor it in later.

Your income will almost certainly be subject to tax. For now, simply put down the amount you receive before or after tax, whichever is easiest. Again, your adviser can help to adjust this for the future.

A note on goals

Many of us have things in life we want to achieve or own – our 'bucket list' goals, or things that feel very important to us. Common examples include major holidays, buying a car, starting a family, buying a house, buying rental properties, taking a sabbatical, funding education (school or further education), renovating a home, paying for a wedding, buying a car – or, like Stephen and Sarah, a camper van. These things all need funding to a greater or lesser extent.

Make a list of the big things you'd like to fund in your life and in three columns add in an idea of the level of funding needed. For most things, when you put your mind to it, there are probably different levels of cost involved. For example, Stephen and Sarah's camper van table looks like this, with three possible levels of expense.

Stephen and Sarah's camper van goal

Goal	Must have	Like to	Dream of!
A camper van to travel to wild beaches in Europe. 	£3,000 a year Could rent one for 2 weeks a year.	£15,000 A second-hand but reliable camper van.	£50,000 A dream camper van straight from the showroom!

Return to table 1 and put all this together with your income and expenses and you'll start to have an idea of the money you have available and what you need to fund.

A broader definition of happiness: the Wheel of Life

While your spending and goals are a great start to the process of creating your personal financial plan, with a little more work on your part it's possible to get even clearer about what makes you happy and therefore what needs to be funded.

Paul J. Meyer was a pioneering businessman, self-help author and motivational speaker who wrote dozens of books about personal development. He's credited with developing an idea that's widely used by life and business coaches to help people think about where they are now and where they want to be in the future.

Meyer's idea is called 'the Wheel of Life'[27]. It starts by asking you to come up with a list of eight areas of life that are important to you.

The Wheel of Life (example)

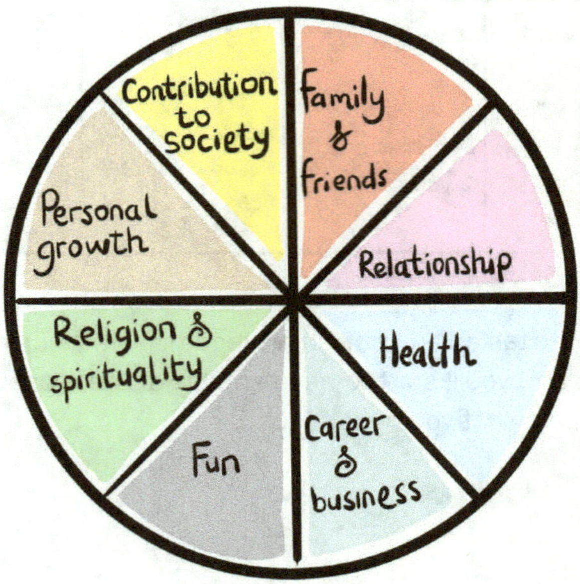

Some ideas to start you off:

- Family
- Friends
- Lifestyle
- Home
- Marriage or relationship
- Health
- Career
- Fun
- Finances
- Contribution to society or your community
- Personal growth
- Religion or spirituality
- Home

You could group some of these under one area (family, friends and your relationship with your partner could all be 'relationships' if you prefer) and you might want to add ideas of your own.

On the blank wheel in Appendix 1, write your eight identified areas on the eight segments. Now ask yourself the following questions.

Where are you today? Simply draw a line on each segment to represent your level of satisfaction with that area. Mark yourself on a scale of one to ten, with one being lowest and closest to the centre of the wheel and ten being the highest level of satisfaction, out on the edge.

Try to do this quickly, going with your gut rather than taking too much time to think about it. At this stage don't worry about *why* you feel things are where they are, just reflect on *where* you think you are.

This is your Wheel of Life. Have a look at it and see if it feels right. You might need two or three attempts. If you haven't thought about things in this way before, then perhaps the categories aren't quite there yet. Is anything missing? Have you captured the broad groups of things that really matter to you? Are you content with your scoring? Once you're happy with it, look at it again.

What's working and what's not working? You probably know this already to some extent, consciously or subconsciously, but having it laid out in this way can be very helpful. Is there anything that surprises you? Are there any areas not getting any or much attention, or any that are getting more attention than you feel they really deserve? Are you devoting so much energy to your career, for example, that you're forgotten to have any fun and spend time with friends and family? Or have you got so comfortable in your leisure time in retirement that you feel like you've stopped growing?

Are you ten out of ten? Once you have drafted your wheel, a great way to refine your picture is to look at each section and ask, 'For me to score this area ten out of ten, what would I be doing? What would I be thinking and feeling?' Note those responses down alongside any goals you have set yourself from the first exercise.

What are the blockers? If some areas on your wheel are working less well, what's holding you back? Perhaps you're in a job or business where you aren't earning enough and can't figure out how to progress. Perhaps your relationship isn't where you want it to be, or you're retired and your friends are drifting away. Do you want to travel more or work less but feel you can't afford it? Make a note of the blockers that are getting in the way. Some of these may be financial, but many will not be. Often, blockers can be a function of time and focus, as well as money and resources.

What action do I need to take? The final step in the Wheel of Life process is to think about what action you need to take to overcome these blockers. For example, if the aim is to advance in your career or business then perhaps a key question is what new skills you need to acquire or who you need to speak to, or if you need to change companies or pivot your business strategy.

You may not be able to address all the blockers immediately, but think about where you'd like to be in the future and how you want to organise your life phases and finances in order to accomplish what you truly want. Once you have the wheel in place, go back to your life phases and your future expenses and check whether anything has changed.

Going deeper: The George Kinder way

George Kinder is the father of life planning, a holistic form of financial planning that aims to help people achieve meaningful lives, rather than simply focusing on money. He has become famous for asking three questions, which I include in full here, with permission, because I've found them so useful in my own life. Thousands of financial advisers from around the globe have been trained in the delivery of these questions[28].

Answering these questions requires the most time and the deepest thinking of the three exercises in this section, but doing so can be extremely rewarding, thought provoking and even life changing. Once you've answered them, look back at the other two exercises. How do they change? How do the dates change? How has your understanding of what you want from the future shifted?

Complete each question before moving on to the next. Kinder's approach is not to read Question 2 until you've completed your answer to Question 1, and so on, so each question has its own page. If you find this approach helpful, have a look at Kinder's book, *Life Planning for You*.

Question 1

I want you to imagine that you are financially secure, that you have enough money to satisfy all of your needs, now and in the future. The question is: how would you live your life? Would you change anything? Let yourself go. Don't hold back on your dreams.

Would you change your life and how would you do it?

Question 2

This time you visit your doctor who tells you that you have five to ten years left to live. The good news is that you won't ever feel sick. The bad news is that you will have no notice of the moment of your death. What will you do in the time you have remaining to live? Your finances remain as they currently stand.

Would you change your life, and how would you do it?

Question 3

This time your doctor shocks you with the news that you only have one day left to live. Notice what feelings arise as you confront your very real mortality. Reflecting on your life, both all your accomplishments to date and all the things you will leave unfinished or undone, ask yourself:

What did I miss?
Who did I not get to be?
What did I not get to do?

Putting it all together

If you've read this chapter and completed the exercises, you should now have a better sense of what happiness looks like for you. The task for you and your adviser now is to work out how to get you there. Even if you've come up with something that feels out of reach, some flexible thinking on both your parts could make it possible.

Let's look at one last example to see why that's the case. Picture a beach at sunset. Three camper vans arrive to take in the view: a brand new Mercedes, bought straight from the forecourt for £50,000; a VW with quite a few miles on the clock, picked up second-hand for £15,000; and a Fiat rented for £2,000 for two weeks. Three couples get out. They set out their tables and chairs and get out their favourite drinks – tea for one, beer for another and champagne for the third. They all settle down to watch the same sunset.

These three couples have very similar visions of happiness: time spent exploring Europe's coastline under their own steam, enjoying natural beauty, each other's company and their favourite drinks. Is the level of happiness achieved any greater for any of the couples? What's different is the amount of money they each had to spend to achieve their vision. This is why understanding what makes you happy in the richest detail possible is important: the amount of money you need to fund the life you want is not fixed; it's variable.

Reflect on your answers and review your must do / like to / dream of table and dates. You are now in a position to share this with your adviser, with a solid foundation from which to build your plan for funding happiness.

Takeaways

1. Think about what makes you happy. Reflect on what happiness means to you personally and how you can fund it in your life. It's all about what brings you joy and fulfilment.
2. Plan with your partner. If you're making future plans with someone else, both of you should independently consider what happiness looks like before coming together to find common ground or make necessary compromises.
3. Sketch your financial future. Create a rough outline of your life phases and financial needs. Think about how your current spending will evolve and include any goals you already have.
4. Use tools to broaden and deepen your view. Try the Wheel of Life to explore different areas of life, and consider George Kinder's three questions to gain a deeper understanding of your desires.
5. Share with your adviser. Once you've got a clearer picture of your happy future, share your thoughts with your financial adviser to start crafting a plan that'll make it happen. Remember, this is about your journey to happiness, so take your time and enjoy the process!

5. What is risk, and why risk it?

Other than her pension, Sarah likes to keep her money in the bank. Having worked hard to earn it, she doesn't want to lose it – and, as we've seen, her childhood experiences have also made her very cautious. Risking her and Stephen's money by investing it in the stock market is a scary and stressful idea.

George, on the other hand, has had quite a lot of experience with investing. Although he had a nice guaranteed pension as a GP, he topped it up with a personal pension and made other investments along the way. But as for many people of his age, George's attitude to taking risk has gradually begun to shift. As his priority has switched from making money to ensuring he doesn't run out of it, he, too, has begun to keep more money in savings accounts.

Sarah and George face the same fundamental challenge: if you don't take risk with your savings, you're certain to lose money over time. Why? Because without investing, you won't be able to access the returns that let you keep pace with inflation – let alone get ahead of it – so the spending power of your money will fall over time. The uncertainty of investing can feel frightening, but what's scarier is the certainty of losing money if you don't.

The good news for those who are nervous about investing is that a lot more is known about investment risk now than even 20 years ago. The science and practice of managing risk for investors has got better and better, and it's now possible to gauge the range of returns, good and bad, you are likely to achieve with different investment types. That makes it much easier to find the right level of risk and the right combination of investments for you – or, to use the analogy from chapter 1, to work out where you should sit on the seesaw.

What is risk and how do we deal with it?

> **THE VALUE OF ADVICE**
> 'Getting used to taking risk takes time. It's often after several years, when they've seen investments fall in value and recover, that clients truly feel more comfortable. However, we're able to help with anxiety along the way, and we're there to talk things through when markets are turbulent.'

Risk is the possibility – but not the certainty – of something bad happening in the future. You can't see the bad thing until it happens, but the potential for it to happen is always there.

Risk may be present, even if you can't see it

Imagine sitting on a sandy beach looking out at a calm sea on a sunny day. Everything looks tranquil as the birds glide on the breeze and the waves gently lap on the shore. But beneath the waves the sea floor drops away to a rock formation that, under certain conditions, can cause a rip tide to form. You can't see it – but the risk is present, nonetheless.

This is what we mean when we talk about risk: the potential for something to go wrong. It doesn't always show itself, but we need to factor it into our plans.

Risk is relative to our experience

In daily life, we get comfortable with taking all kinds of risk – when we cross the road, drive on the motorway or get on a plane. We learn to manage these everyday risks: by looking both ways before we cross the road, checking the tyre pressure before a long journey or flying with a reputable airline. We also learn to cope with uncertainty about the things we can't manage: the speeding motorbike, the jack-knifed lorry, the engine failure.

We deal better with risks that are part of our daily experience. Someone used to driving through country lanes might find the volume and noise of city traffic unsettling. Equally, a city driver might find narrow country lanes and blind corners terrifying. A news story about an airline accident would be more likely to cause a sleepless night for someone about to fly for the first time than someone who flies for business every week.

It's the same with investing. Academic research based on Dynamic Planner data shows that those who invest get more comfortable with risk over time[29]. In fact, the longer they invest for, up to a certain point, the more willing they are to take more risk.

If the size of a football pitch represents the number of adults in the UK (around 60 million people), then the number of UK adults who invest (around 8 million people) would fit into a single penalty area[30]. You can see that investors are still very much in the minority: it's not a very common experience. Compare that to the almost 36 million people who would watch a Premier

League football match on TV: they would fill over half the pitch[31].

While the number of investors is growing, particularly through pension savings (there are 17 million investors in the UK if you include everyone who invests through their workplace pensions too), it's still not mainstream – and we certainly don't talk about our experience of investing as much as we do about the match at the weekend! If we do hear about it, it's often because something has gone wrong. As a result, those starting out tend to be more concerned about the risks of investing than excited about the benefits.

But think about how you learned to manage other risks. If you're a regular driver, you probably now navigate motorways with ease – but you once had to learn how to turn the car on. You had lessons, or someone who sat in the car with you and showed you how it was done, and you started with slower roads so you could gradually build your skills. Today, everything you do to stay safe has become second nature. You accept that there's some risk, but you control the elements you can and live with the rest.

As with driving, most of the risks of investing can be managed with a degree of certainty. And with a financial adviser, you have a highly experienced instructor to take you on the journey. Over four million people now take investment advice in the UK from professional advisers. And we know that when they do, their confidence about investing grows[32].

How we evaluate risk – and why the past isn't always a great guide

While experience of investing is helpful, risk isn't something you can always spot by looking at the past. Going back to our beach example: for the last nine days all has been quiet, with gentle winds and calm seas. It would be easy to conclude that it's always safe to swim. On the tenth day, though, the wind gets up, the current shifts and a rip tide forms. A local lifeguard might recognise the conditions and encourage swimmers to stay out of the water that day, but someone basing their decision solely on what had happened in their holiday so far might not notice the shift in conditions.

It's the same with investing. Investments can show their risks all the time, or they can go a long time – sometimes years – without showing them. But then conditions change and, like the rocks, the characteristics that were always there cause the risk to materialise.

One of the most profound challenges for investors the world over is that traditional measures of investment risk are mostly backwards looking, describing what the risk *was* yesterday, but not what it *will be* today or tomorrow. If nothing went wrong over that period – in our beach example, on days one to nine – then the risk might look very low.

Equally, you can't obtain a complete picture by looking at the average. Without getting into the maths behind averages, we saw that nine days out of ten, it was safe to swim at that beach – and those might sound like good odds: 90% safe. On the tenth day, though, the risk was extreme, and you would have had to have very good water skills to stay afloat.

Does that mean risk can't be measured – that if you choose to invest you'll be taking a step into the complete unknown? No. The good news is that much better ways of understanding risk have evolved, particularly over the last two decades. The approach set out in this book uses these techniques to form an assessment of future risks – a more useful guide than relying on history.

Why take investment risk at all?

Risk, then, is the possibility of something bad happening – and all of us get used to dealing with that in various ways in our daily lives, but we've seen that investment risk can feel particularly scary because many of us aren't used to it at all.

Maybe, like Sarah, we've got by without it until now. But if we want to fund happiness and we don't want our money to run out in the process, it's another kind of risk we'll need to get comfortable with.

Let's take a closer look at why that is.

Money buys you less over time: Number of slices of bread for 8p

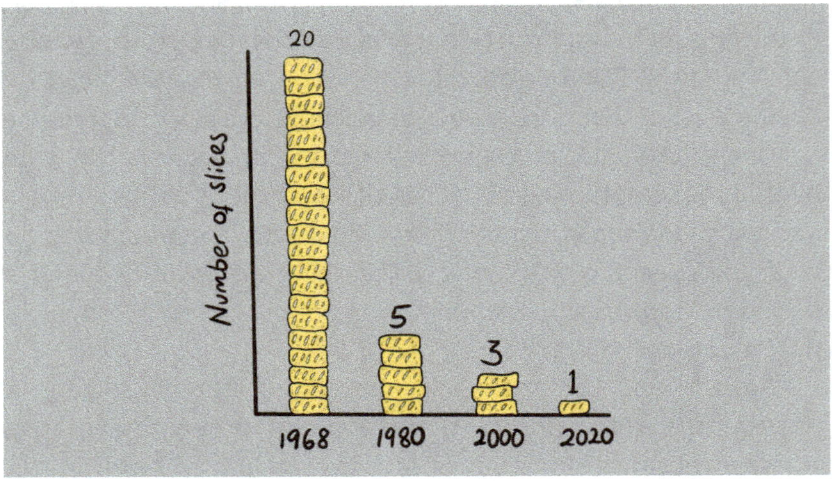

Back in 1968, the average price of a loaf of bread with 20 slices was only eight pence. Eight pence for a loaf of bread! Inflation in the 1970s was so high that, had bread been sold by the slice, by 1980 your eight pence would barely have bought you five slices. By 2000, that was down to just three slices. And today? You would only get a single slice. At the time of writing, the average price of a white sliced loaf is £1.60.

Prices rise over the years, and that means the value of your savings can quickly be eroded. The money that Sarah and George had intended to see them safely through retirement might not pay for their lifestyle for long.

Even a relatively low level of inflation – for example, 2%, the target level for the Bank of England and other central banks around the world – eats away at your savings over time. Let's say Sarah has £100,000 just sitting in the bank. In ten years' time, assuming inflation of 2%, the buying power of her money would have fallen to the equivalent of £82,000 today. In 20 years' time, it would be down to £67,000. While taking risk with the family's money might feel uncertain to Sarah, she faces the certainty of losing money if she doesn't.

How to invest to beat inflation and get the returns you need – the basics

So how do you beat inflation and get the returns you need to fund the life you want? In a nutshell: by investing your money. As a general rule, the greater the risk you take, the greater *the potential* for return. That's not the same as saying you're guaranteed to get a greater return if you take more risk. However, over the long term you stand a much greater chance of doing so.

How money flows through the economy

To see why more risk increases your return potential, it's helpful to understand how money works its way through the economy.

When you put your money in the bank, you receive a relatively small amount of interest (your 'return') – which is acceptable to you because your money is protected by the bank and easy to get hold of. The bank is prepared to pay you interest in exchange for holding your savings because it knows it can lend your money out – and the return it makes will more than cover the cost of its interest payments to you, because it will charge a higher rate of interest on the loans.

Imagine now that one of those loans goes to a landlord who wants to buy an office building. She's willing to pay interest on the loan because she's confident she can get more in rent than she needs to cover both the cost of the loan and her other costs, and also make a profit.

She then rents the building out to a business looking for more space. The business owner rents the building because he believes he can make more money from the business than is needed to cover both the rent and his other costs, and also make a profit.

He funds his business by taking out a loan, on which he has to pay a higher rate of interest than the landlord's property loan because his business is riskier and the loan isn't secured on a property. The loan also needs to be repaid over time. Instead of a bank loan, bigger companies might borrow money by issuing bonds – a way of borrowing from investors.

How money flows

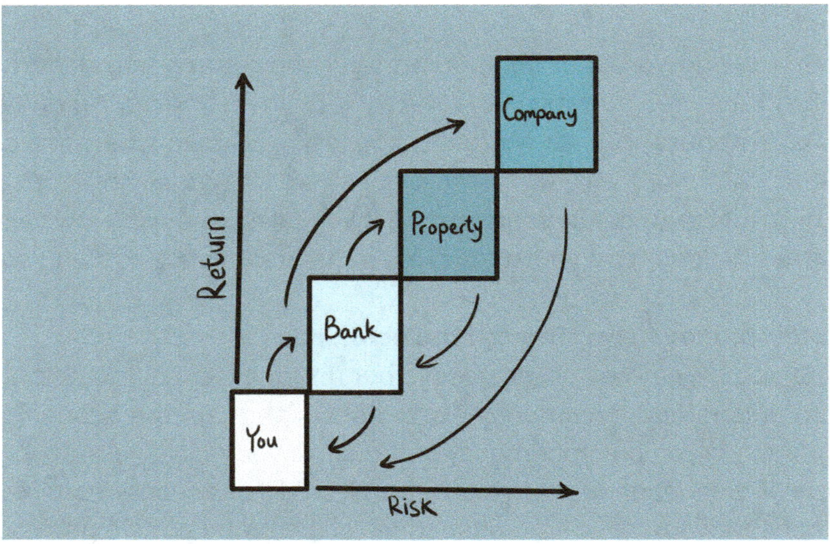

As the business grows, he funds its expansion by getting people to invest directly as shareholders. Those shareholders expect to get a higher return than the lenders who lent the company money, because – unlike a loan – their investment does not have to be repaid. Instead, they hope to make a profit when they sell their shares, and also perhaps receive a share of the company's profits, in the form of dividends, while they hold the shares.

Along this chain, certainty about the future diminishes, and so risk increases, but so does the potential return.

As well as individuals and companies, governments participate in this chain, funding their own investments – for example, in hospitals and schools – by raising money through loans or bonds. In the UK, the government is seen as a safe bet, so government bonds (known as 'gilts') have a lower interest rate than bonds issued by companies.

As an individual, you can choose where to participate in this chain, or you can invest in several different parts of it. The task is to maximise the return you can achieve at a risk that's right for you *and no more*. We'll talk more about how to do this effectively later in the book.

The relationship between risk and return

Impact of inflation on cash over the last 20 years (£1,000 initial investment)

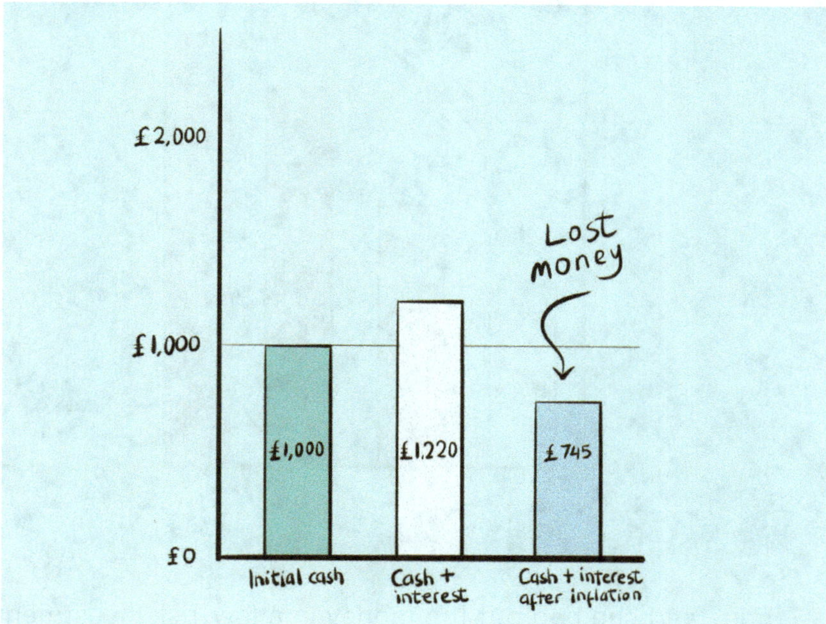

Dynamic Planner has measured the risk and return of the different investments available to investors in the UK for the last 20 years. While history is not a reliable guide to future investment choices, it can provide a good illustration of how the relationship between risk and return works.

Let's assume Sarah had £1,000 to save 20 years ago. If she'd put the money in a savings account, she'd now have £1,220. The effect of inflation, though, means her money is now actually worth less (in terms of how much bread it would buy) than when she started – a real value (adjusted for inflation) of just £745. Savings in the bank will lose you money over time.

Impact of investing over the last 20 years (£1,000 initial investment)

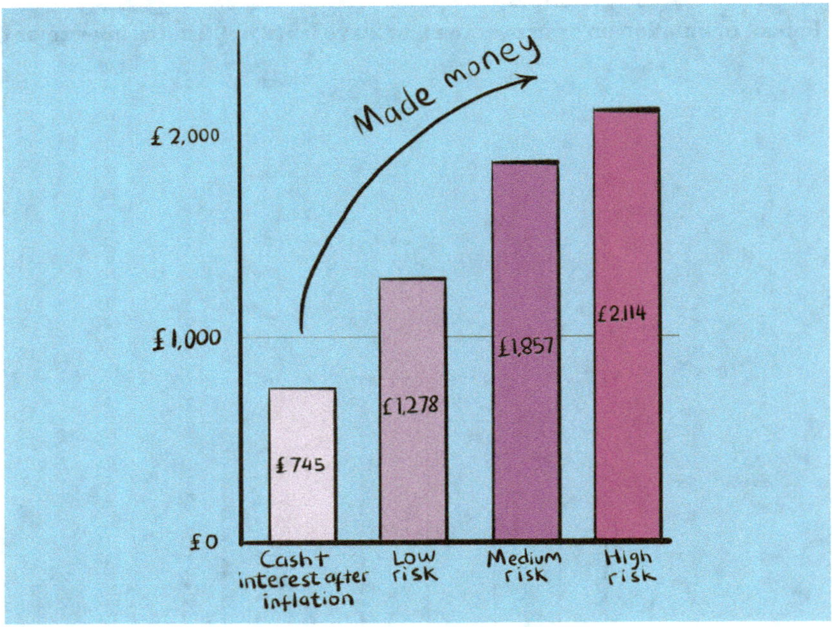

If instead she had put the money in a low-risk investment (such as bonds), her £1,000 would be worth £1,278 after the effects of inflation.

If she'd invested it in a medium-risk investment made up mostly of bonds, property and some shares, she'd have £1,857 after inflation today. In a high-risk investment, made up mostly of shares, she would have £2,114.

Over the 20-year period, the more risk you took, the more money you would have made. Study after study, looking at different markets at different times, shows the same thing: *taking more risk with your investments in a structured and diversified way* (we'll say more about this later) *puts you in a position where you are more likely to gain a higher return over the long term.* That's why investors take risk.

What about the ups and downs? Sarah likes to keep her money in the bank because, while it won't make a lot, the number she sees when she checks her balance will never be smaller than it was the last time she looked. This feeling is common to many of us and is often why people decide not to invest.

So let's see what the bad days looked like along the way.

The initial £1,000 in cash savings didn't fall in value in absolute terms – although don't forget the real value of cash savings after inflation was £745 at the end of the 20 years.

At one point, the low-risk investment fell to £988. The medium-risk investment's lowest point was £862 and the high-risk investment's lowest point during the 20 years was £853. All these figures are before the effects of inflation.

The more risk you took, the greater the biggest fall in value you would have seen, as well as the greater the rise by the end of the period.

Lowest value over the last ten years (£1,000 initial investment)

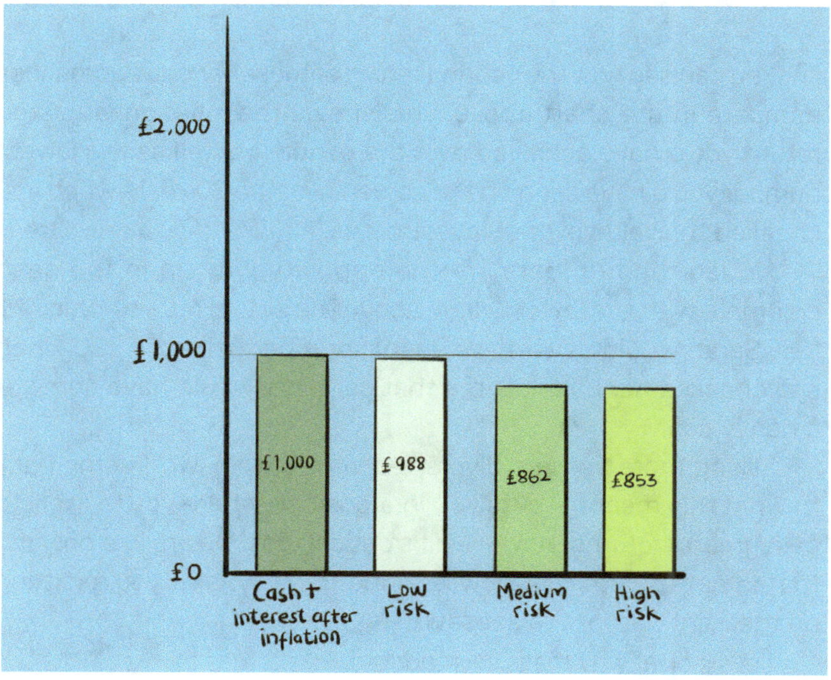

How risk and return have compared over the last 20 years (£1,000 initial investment)

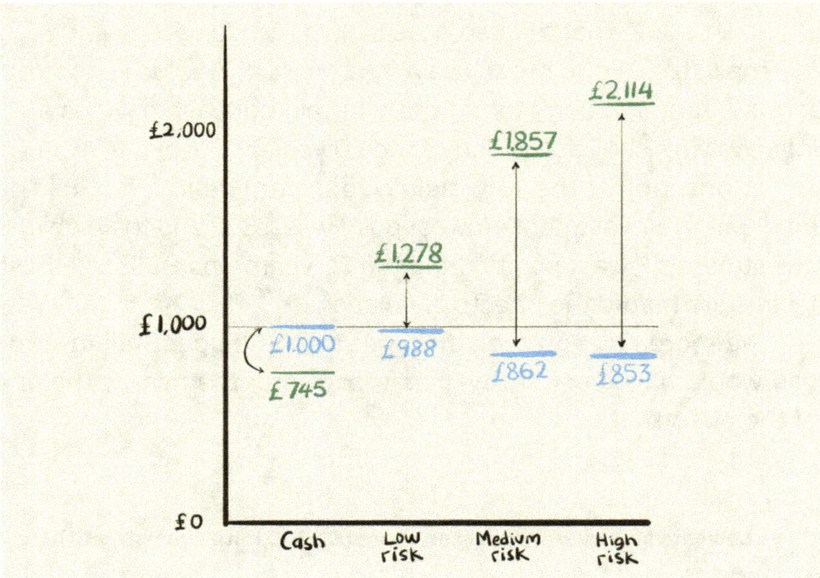

You can see how the risk and return of these various approaches compare in the chart above. This shows the inflation-adjusted return you'd have achieved over the period, as well as the lowest number you'd have seen on the screen over the 20 years when you checked the value of your investments.

Notice the numbers are the opposite way up in the cash column – with the lowest value above the actual return achieved. Yes, Sarah would never have seen a number below £1,000 when she checked her balance, but that certainty would have come at a heavy cost.

Taking more risk in a diversified way – again, we'll come back to what this means – puts you in a position where you're likely to gain greater returns. However, it's critical that you are in a position to ride out the ups and downs along the way: that you're sitting on the right part of the seesaw.

Let's look at why that's so important.

Why how you feel about risk matters

> **THE VALUE OF ADVICE**
> 'Many people's perception of any investment other than cash is that their money could halve overnight. By looking at portfolios at the client's chosen risk level with the charting tools we have available today, we can clearly demonstrate that that's not the case.'

One reason investors fail to achieve their goals is that they take more risk than they are comfortable with, can't tolerate the bumpy ride and sell their investments when they are falling or low in value. Once you sell an investment, that's it: any losses are locked in and there's no chance to recover the lost money. If Sarah had opted for the low-, medium- or high-risk investments but then sold them at their lowest point over the past ten years, she wouldn't have benefited from the subsequent recoveries.

How we feel about investing makes a big difference to our success. And even if it all feels logical as you read this chapter, it can feel very different in the heat of the moment, when the press, blogs and news outlets are pumping out good news ('markets are up, profits are up, the latest investments are up') or bad news ('stock market crises around the world, companies are going bankrupt, industries are failing') 24 hours a day. In the heat of a boom or the teeth of a crisis, making good rational investment choices can be more difficult than it seems.

One of the central roles of a financial adviser is to be the steady hand throughout the market's ups and downs – encouraging you to think long term, keep calm in turbulent times and not take too much or indeed too little risk, just because of recent fluctuations.

Psychologists have studied investor emotions extensively around the world in relation to stock market cycles. Check in with your own feelings about investment as you're reading this chapter. Where do you sit in the cycle?

How emotions can affect investment decision making

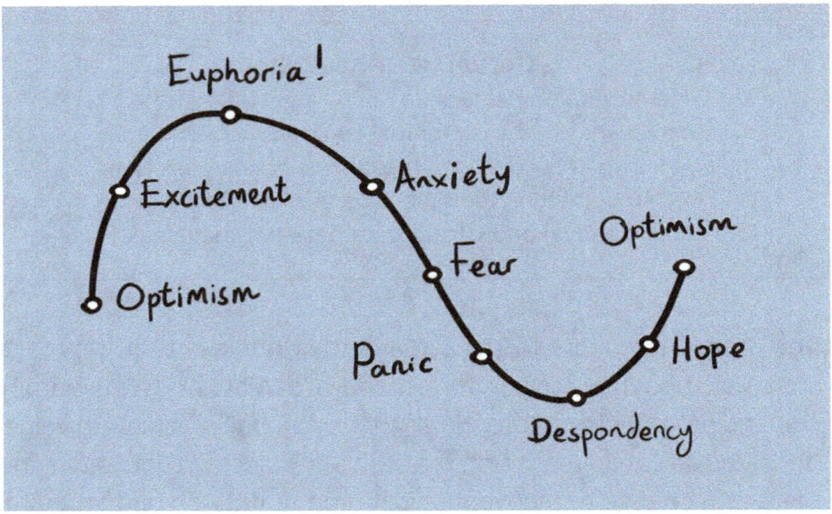

When markets are on the rise, we're keener to invest, experiencing optimism and excitement as investments grow in value. But that means we can end up buying when prices are high. If markets fall, emotions can turn to denial, fear and even panic as we see investment values plummet, along with our expectations. As a result, investors can end up selling when prices are low. If you're experiencing these emotions, you're not alone.

Just like with driving or flying, over time, with experience, we get more comfortable with investment risk – if it's at the right level for us and we don't go too far too fast. It's easy to imagine that if Sarah had ignored her misgivings and gone for the high-risk investments, she might not have held her nerve as a first-time investor, but perhaps the low- or medium-risk investments might have felt okay, particularly if she'd had a financial adviser by her side to reassure her in the difficult periods.

An adviser will work with you to establish the right level of risk for you. They can monitor your investments to make sure you're taking that risk and no more – and if you get more confident and feel ready to increase the risk, they can help you make the change.

What might go wrong

Finally, it's worth a note on the fear of the unknown – a big contributor to concerns about investing. Let's look at some of the most frequent questions people have for their advisers on the subject.

- **Could I lose everything?** This is the secret fear of many first-time investors like Sarah, and while it would be a very bad outcome, it's highly preventable. This book is about making the kind of sensible financial decisions, with a financial adviser, that make losing everything very unlikely.

- **Could I lose my initial investment?** The initial amount you invest will fluctuate to a greater or lesser extent depending on the investments you choose. Today, financial advisers can explain your range of likely returns or losses even in very unusual circumstances – and if you're not comfortable, you can change something.

- **What happens if I don't achieve the return I want?** To minimise the risk of a surprise at the end of the road, it's important that you and your adviser keep checking in on your progress and adjusting your plan as needed to keep you on track. It may be that you need to invest more, change the level of risk you are taking or invest for longer. But regular reviews at least once a year are the way to manage this as you go.

- **Can I lose more than I can afford**? The process of professional investment advice is all about putting you into a situation where this is much less likely to happen. All professional advisers will do their utmost to ensure it never happens. With your adviser, you will think carefully about what you can afford to lose and factor that carefully into your plan. Reviewing this number every so often (once a year or if your circumstances change) is the best way to stay on top of things.

- **What if I get a bad run when I start investing?** This is a tough hand to be dealt. Even if you're planning to invest for years, if your investments fall a lot in value early on, it's not only psychologically challenging but it can take you a longer time to recover your initial value. If you have a lump sum to invest and markets are bumpy, it might be better to drip-feed it gradually into the markets rather than investing it all at once, to help to reduce this risk.

- **What if markets are low when I need my money**? You and your adviser will plan your exit strategy as carefully as the rest of the journey – including your income requirements and any big life events you might need money for. It starts with understanding your priorities, being clear on your needs and ensuring you have a sufficient buffer in place.

- **What if there's another market crash?** You might have heard big stock market crashes described as 'one in a hundred year storms' or 'Black Swan' events[33]. Markets have always recovered over the long term, so the best strategy is to build a plan that can handle the fluctuations you can expect the vast majority of the time. In very extreme circumstances, a crash or crisis might mean you have to keep investing for longer. Ensuring that you have the capacity to do this will be key to your plan.

- **Will I invest in unregulated investments like crypto?** The mainstream ways of investing recommended by financial advisers are regulated in the UK by the Financial Conduct Authority (FCA). Beyond these regulated investments, the risks of investing are less well understood; there just isn't the long-term data. Investments like cryptocurrencies are still in their infancy and currently offer nothing in the way of investor protection. In other words, this type of investing is the Wild West. A financial adviser won't recommend this approach and is unlikely to be able to help you with it. If you choose to dip in, make sure you do it with money you can afford to lose.

Why is it helpful to think about all these things now? Because it's easier to deal with lots of smaller, more specific dangers than one vast and unknowable one. And because identifying the risks is the first step to managing them.

Engaging with your adviser is key. The days of buying an investment and putting it away for 25 years only to find that it's not on course to pay off the mortgage, for example, are well and truly behind us. If you have a well-built financial plan and you and your adviser engage to check on progress, you're better placed to manage risks when they do appear and in the best place you can be to achieve the returns you need to fund happiness.

Takeaways

1. Risk is the possibility of something bad happening in the future. It can always be present but doesn't always show up. You can't measure it by looking at the past, and averages won't give you the full picture.
2. Risk is relative to your experience. We get comfortable with taking all kinds of risks in daily life, such as crossing the road or flying. Similarly, with investing, the more you do it, the more comfortable you will become with the risks involved and how to manage them.
3. Traditional measures of investment risk are mostly backward-looking. They describe what the risk was yesterday but not today. It's important to use better ways of understanding risk that provide a forward-looking view.
4. If you don't take risks with your savings, you're certain to lose money over time due to inflation. Investments help you keep pace with inflation and ideally to beat it.
5. How you feel about investing really matters. If you don't feel comfortable on the investment journey, you might not stay the course. As humans we're all emotional creatures and it's difficult to make fully rational decisions in good markets or bad. An adviser can help you maintain a steady course.

6. How to use risk to increase your returns

We've already looked at the corrosive impact of inflation on your wealth. Some economists call it 'the silent assassin', reducing the value of your money year in, year out, unless you take action against it. But even keeping pace with inflation almost certainly won't be enough to fund the life you want (unless you're in the small minority of people who have already accumulated sufficient assets for a lifetime).

Aisha's just turned 35 and has no retirement plans whatsoever – she has her life ahead of her. She was auto-enrolled in her company's pension scheme and has built up a small pension pot, but when she goes freelance she will need to make her own provisions.

The good news is she has time on her side. But even if you've left it later, there are still ways to fund the life you want – if you're prepared to take some risk to get there. And you have a powerful friend in the form of a phenomenon called compounding.

Why not leave my money in the bank?

While Aisha isn't thinking about retirement, the age at which she can draw her state pension is currently 68. This is the point at which she will need to rely on that pension, plus what she has saved.

Aisha has sensibly built up an emergency fund – a good rule of thumb for this is enough to cover about three to six months of expenses, in an easy-access account. With some help from her family, she's also managed to get together enough for a house deposit. She's aware that she needs some provision for the future, so she saves £100 per month and puts it in the bank. A reasonable long-term average saving rate for this is around 1% a year. By the time she's 68, Aisha will have saved around £51,643, including interest.

The average UK household spends £32,000 a year[34], so assuming no other form of income, the money she has saved would last her about a year and a half.

But the situation is actually worse, because we haven't factored in the impact of inflation. All the time Aisha is trying to fund happiness, the silent assassin is quietly working against her, eating away at her buying power as prices rise. If we factor in 2% inflation, the savings from Aisha's £100 a month would actually run out in less than a year.

As we've seen, it's good practice these days to plan to live until 90 or even 100, unless you have clear health reasons to expect otherwise. In other words, Aisha is currently falling well short of what she needs for a happy retirement.

What are her options? She either needs to save a lot more money each month to allow for future inflation or find a better return on the money she is putting away.

The wonder of compounding

This time, rather than putting her £100 in the bank. Aisha decides to take some risk and invest her money. The return for the average UK investor is just over 5% a year[35]. You can, of course, get more than 5%, but that means taking more risk. The highest level of return an individual investor in the UK might reasonably expect to achieve over the long run is about 8.5% a year, but that level of return creates a very bumpy journey, with the value of your money rising and falling a lot along the way. So let's stick with the average of 5%.

With a return of 5% a year, Aisha's £100 a month gives her £116,000 by the time she hits retirement age, well over double what she'd have if she left her money the bank. With inflation factored in, that would last her about two years – more than twice as long as her bank account savings, but not long enough.

What can Aisha do to change this situation? Four things – which, combined, can make a big difference.

- **Increase the amount she saves** a bit each year as her earnings rise. Wages tend to rise a bit faster than prices, and Aisha plans to increase her freelance rates accordingly, so let's assume she can afford to invest 5% more each year. In the first year, she invests £100 a month; in the second, she invests £105 ... and so on. Now, when she retires, she has £225,000 – that small change makes a big difference.

- On top of that, she could **take more risk**. Aisha is young enough that the ups and downs associated with riskier investments won't impact her lifestyle, as she won't be accessing the money for many years. (We'll see later how your adviser can help you work out how much risk you're willing and able to take.) It's more important to maximise her returns than to have a smooth investment journey. So she chooses a risk level that's expected to provide an average long-term return of around 7%. This means that by the time she is 68 she can plan for her pot to be around £320,000. Now after inflation this still only funds five years in retirement, so what else can she do?

- She can **invest for longer**. If she continues to work until she's 75, her pot would reasonably be around £600,000. If, on top of that, she could increase her savings level by 7% a year instead of 5%, this number would be closer to £850,000. We will look at why these numbers grow so quickly later in this chapter. After inflation, this pot might last her for 12 years or so, funding the same lifestyle until she was 87: much closer to what she wants.

- Aisha figures that she won't actually need to fund everything she pays for today in retirement, either. The mortgage will be paid off and Sammy will have grown up. So perhaps she will **spend less**. If she did, that she could stretch her savings to around her mid-90s – a good age to plan to.

How to make the maths work

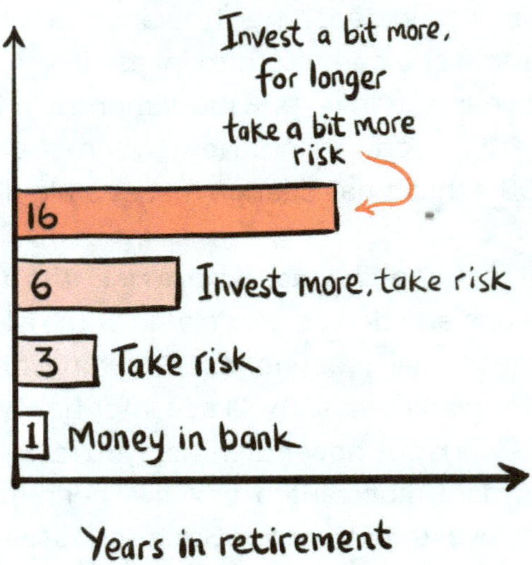

You can see the really big differences that taking more risk and giving yourself more time can make. Aisha goes from one to 12 years of funding for retirement by simply putting a bit more of her money into higher returning investments and giving them more time to grow.

Why is there such a difference? It's because of something called 'compounding'.

Picture rolling a snowball downhill. As it rolls, it picks up snow. With each roll, more snow clings to the snow from the previous roll and so the snowball gets larger. The bigger it gets, the larger the surface area and the more snow it gathers. The snowball keeps getting bigger and bigger, and the longer it continues to roll, the bigger it gets.

The snowball is your money. When you invest it, it attracts investment returns. Those returns become part of the snowball, which gathers yet more returns as it goes. If you attract higher returns, the surface area of your snowball gets bigger faster, and those returns gather returns, and so on. After a while, the difference really begins to show.

The power of compounding

That's why investing for longer is transformative for Aisha. Towards the end of her investment journey, her snowball is already very big, so letting it roll for longer makes a huge difference.

That's also why investing earlier in life can be so powerful. If Aisha had started saving £100 a month when she was 21, increasing it by 5% a year and achieving a return of 7%, she could plan on having over a million by the age of 68!

Making sure that you're taking the right amount of risk – which, if you have the capacity and time on your side, could be a little more than you might initially feel comfortable with – and then giving yourself as much time as possible are the keys to making compounding work for you.

Yes, but I'm not 21 any more

Of course, many of us are not 21 any more – and many 21 year olds are too focused on the immediate challenges of building a life for themselves to think about funding future happiness.

We've seen what you do if you're 35, but what about if you're 50 or over and you haven't made much of a provision for the future?

The good news is that you still have time to make compounding your friend. If you like a bit of maths, a useful way to think about it is the rule of 70 – an easy calculation to help you work out where you can get to from where you are today. Simply put, if you divide 70 by the return on your investment, the answer is the number of years it will take for your money to double. So if you receive a 5% return, you can double your money in 14 years (70 ÷ 5). If you get a 7% return, you can double it in 10 years (70 ÷ 7). Returns matter!

Let's say you're 50 and you have £100,000 in savings. If you left that money in the bank, it would take until you were 120 to double it to £200,000 – not happening! If you invest it with a 5% return before inflation, you can double it by the time you're 64.

If you increase your risk to a level with an average 7% return, you could double your £100,000 to £200,000 by the time you're 60, and again to £400,000 by the time you're 70.

Importantly, you should only take as much risk as you're comfortable with. But hopefully you can see that there are routes available to you. And could you work a bit longer, save a bit more, and reduce your expenses? Then add in the state pension – £10,000 per person per year at the time of writing – and it starts to feel liveable[36].

What if you're 50 and you don't have a lump sum to invest? Can you afford to put some money away every month? If you invested £1,000 a month from the age of 50 to 65, you'd have almost £300,000 by age 64 and £460,000 – or 20+ years of living expenses – by age 70. That might still feel out of reach – but you can get to the same place by putting away £400 a month this year and increasing the amount you save by just 10% a year. It's not at all uncommon for people in their 50s and 60s to have to make 'uncomfortable levels of savings' – forgoing spending to invest as much as they can into their pension to fund the life they want when they retire. This is a common scenario for advisers, and something they'll know how to help you with.

Many people avoid thinking about retirement because it feels like it's too early or too late. But you can hopefully begin to see that there are options, wherever you are in life. And the best time to start is now.

THE VALUE OF ADVICE

'It's not unusual at all for clients to really start to think hard about preparing for life in retirement in their 50s or even 60s. Because of other commitments – children, education, divorce, health concerns – it may well be that there is a lot of catching up to do in this period to help ensure security of lifestyle in retirement. The good news is that through a combination of sometimes uncomfortable saving, taking a slightly higher level of risk with investments and letting time and the power of compounding do its thing, a lot of clients do achieve the outcomes they are looking for.'

What if I'm already in or close to retirement?

For some people, the realisation that at some point they'll need to slow down or stop working comes early in their careers, allowing lots of time for planning and saving. For others, it comes later. On average, people get to grips with the serious business of preparing for retirement between the ages of 55 and 75.

At this point, the wealth people have available to them varies widely, from very little to a lot. Sarah and Stephen have around £300,000 in a combination of pensions and ISAs – the average for those who seek advice today at their age[37].

If you're in this group, often your most pressing question for your adviser will be 'When can I afford to retire?' – or, to put it another way, 'If I retired and stopped earning money, how long would my money last?'

Let's assume Stephen and Sarah can live on about two-thirds of the average UK household income (£35,000) in retirement – say, £24,000 a year. To keep things simple and focus on what compounding can achieve for them, we'll ignore their state pensions and other assets such as equity in their home.

- If Sarah and Stephen both stopped working today, put their £300,000 in the bank and took out £24,000 a year, they would run out of money after 12 years. Because prices will increase over that time, their standard of living will fall, as £24,000 at the end of the period won't buy what it did at the start. That might mean they take out more money earlier and run out sooner.

- If they invest the money, taking medium risk (in Dynamic Planner, we call this risk level 5 out of 10), they could plan, on average, to benefit from a 5% return (before inflation) over the long term and their money should last almost 18 years on average, taking them to ages 72 and 67.

The best way to make your money last as long as possible is to get higher returns for longer. That means taking some investment risk in retirement. The balance between the risk you're willing and able to take and the money you need to withdraw to fund the lifestyle you want is one of the most important conversations to have with an adviser.

Planning around averages

You might notice that so far in this chapter we've used the term 'average' quite a lot. You might also remember from when we talked about the nature of risk that averages hide a great deal – 90% of the time, it was safe to swim at the beach with the hidden rocks, but 10% of the time it was potentially disastrous.

Very few people actually achieve the average return. Most people will gain a little more or a little less, and a few people will gain considerably more or considerably less. Even when you do achieve the average growth rate over time, your path there is highly unlikely to be a straight line.

Over decades, strong relationships have been formed between the level of risk in a well-constructed, globally diversified investment solution and the returns you can expect over the long term. Along the way, though, they'll meander around the average a little to a lot. And the more risk you take, the bigger these ups and downs are likely to be.

Planning around the average

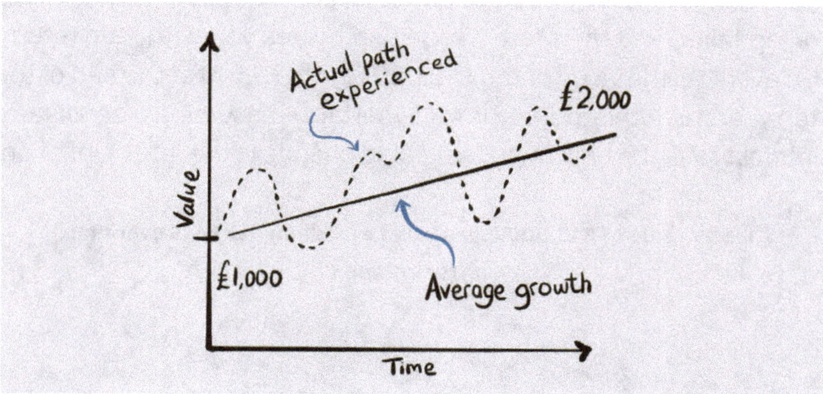

Something your adviser will want you to avoid on your investment journey is surprises. Surprises can make people panic, and panic often means we lose money by selling investments we would be better off holding onto. To illustrate the power of compounding, we've kept things simple so far by talking about the *average* expected return for each journey we've looked at. But when we're thinking about your money, it's more useful to talk about a range of potential outcomes.

Likely value of £10,000 cash in the bank over time, after inflation

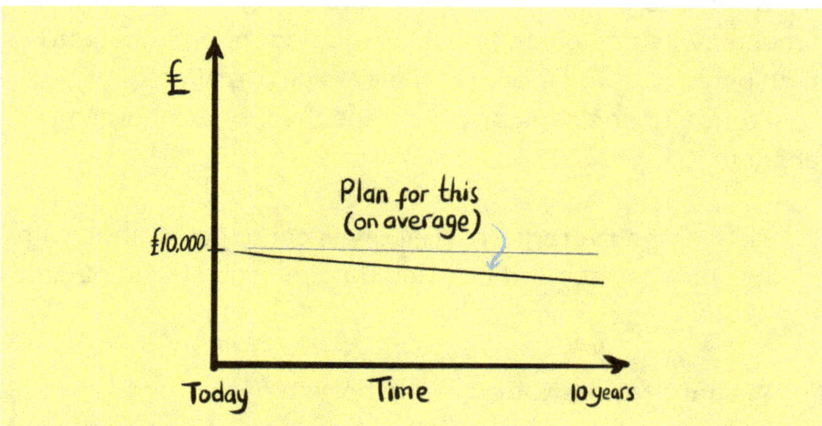

As we have already seen, the real value of your money in the bank *falls* over time once inflation is taken into account. Little risk is being taken and therefore the bank provides you with little return. On average, the value of the £10,000 falls to £7,810 at the end of the ten years. But this journey is quite certain – assuming a consistent interest rate, the only thing that could change is the rate of inflation.

Likely value of £10,000 invested at a medium risk level over time, after inflation

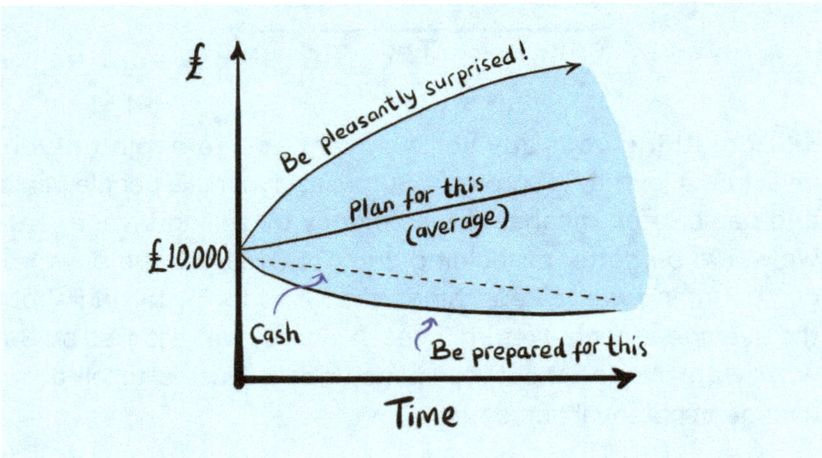

When you invest, it's different. To capture the uncertainty around averages, we can project a corridor of potential returns, both better and worse, around the average over time.

From a financial planning perspective, here's how to think about that:

1. Plan for the **average** value – but expect to get a return within the 'corridor' somewhere. Half the time you should be pretty close to the average.

2. **Prepare for** the values at the bottom of the corridor – build your plan so you know what to do if this were to happen.

Technically, 95% of the years you are invested, you should get a return above this line. But that said, 5% of the time, or one in 20 years, you may not. Your adviser will want to talk to you about what you would do in these circumstances. The best answer, if at all possible, is to stay invested until your investments are back closer to their long-term average[38].

3. Finally, you might be **pleasantly surprised** and achieve more than the average return.

The chart above shows how that looks if you invest at a medium risk profile (5 out of 10). The shaded area is the corridor of potential returns. The things to look at here are:

1. The **average return** is expected to deliver a positive return for you after inflation, and perform better than cash.

2. The corridor is much wider, reflecting a greater range of potential returns, both higher and lower. Interestingly, though, the '**be prepared for this**' line is only just below what you might expect, on average, from cash after inflation. This is an important dynamic to understand – that *the vast majority of the time you should expect to beat cash over the long term*, even in bad markets.

3. The **pleasantly surprised** line is much higher, reflecting the fact that from time to time on stock markets you can get quite large positive returns considerably above the average, albeit less frequently[39]. But it's best to disregard this, focus on the average return over the long term and be surprised if you get a better outcome.

For people who like numbers, Appendix 2 includes a table of Dynamic Planner estimates at the time of publication. These change over time, but can give you a good feel for the different range of returns you can expect for different risk profiles.

The possible paths through the corridor are infinite

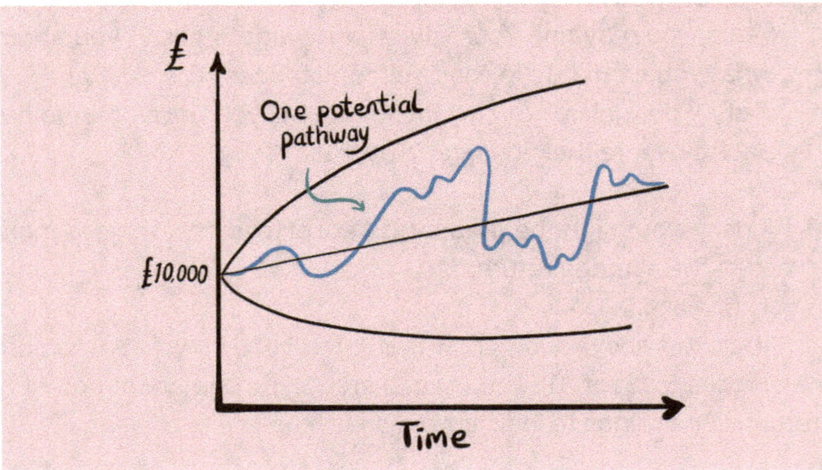

The final thing to note is that there are an infinite number of pathways through the corridor. Most of the types of investment you might invest in are priced daily, and that price can move around each day a little or a lot. In the pathway in the diagram, the investment is operating within the corridor and around the average, but with a lot of daily, monthly and annual variance. The more risk you take, the more movement you are likely to see in your returns.

To state the obvious, your adviser can't control future returns any more than they can control the weather. What they can and will do is to ensure the risk you take is managed in line with the risk you agree with them – a bit like telling a taxi driver how fast they are allowed to go to get you from A to B. Given that risk, when properly used, is the main driver of return, this is the key thing to manage. Using software, an adviser will be able to model your situation and the risk you are taking to illustrate your potential corridor of returns.

Takeaways

1. Money in the bank is not only exposed to the 'silent assassin' of inflation, but almost certainly won't be enough to fund the life you want – particularly in retirement.
2. Compounding is a powerful ally. Like a snowball rolling down a hill, your initial investment gathers returns, and those returns gather more returns.
   More time and higher returns increase the benefits.
3. Taking some risk with your money is necessary. Your adviser will help you work out how much you can afford and how much you're willing to take.
4. It's never too late to start – whether you're 21, 35 or over 50, there are routes to get you where you want to go. But starting earlier gives your investments more time to make the most of compounding.
5. The average return is only a guide. Plan for a range of returns, not one single outcome, and don't expect a straight line. The more risk you take, the bigger the likely ups and downs along the way.

7. The risks to the planet

George has the future of the planet on his mind. He flies to Australia every year to see his daughter and grandchildren and he's started to feel bad about those air miles. He doesn't want to miss out on seeing them, but he wants his grandchildren to grow up in a safe and hospitable world. He's begun to look at what else he could change.

One potential area is his investments. He needs them to give him a return that will make sure his money doesn't run out, but at the same time he wants that money to be doing more good than harm. Is that possible?

Aisha, in common with many people of her generation, would describe herself as worried about climate change. She talks about it with friends, and it sometimes keeps her awake at night. At work, she ran a project for a client who makes solar technology for renewable energy, so she also knows there are some exciting solutions out there.

Sustainability might be something you haven't thought about in relation to funding your future life, or it might be a question that's top-of-mind for you. If it feels like something you want to factor in, you're not alone – as we saw back in chapter 1, about two-thirds of financial advisers' clients place 'some' to 'very high' importance on the sustainability of their investments, while only a third see it of 'low' importance.

We'll look at how an adviser can help you think through where you are on this spectrum in chapter 9. Wherever you land – whether you want to extend the environmentally conscious choices you make in other areas of your life to your investments, or your priorities are elsewhere – climate change represents both one of the single biggest risks to your investments and is one of the biggest investment opportunities of our lifetimes.

The sustainable investor's dilemma

Sustainability is one of the most complex and hotly debated topics in the investment world. Not only the importance investors want to or should place on it, but also, *how* they should invest sustainably—and what does 'investing sustainably' even mean? There are very few widely agreed definitions and even when there are, there are still nuances and trade-offs to think through.

Take the apparently simple case of investing in oil and gas companies. On the one hand, they are producers of fossil fuels, which ultimately release the greenhouse gases that warm the atmosphere and change the climate. Through this lens, they are to be avoided if you want to invest sustainably.

But on the other hand, we still need their power to fuel the transition to renewables—to build the electric cars, forge the wind turbines and manufacture the hydroelectric power stations of the future. And, in the short to medium term, we need their power to keep the lights on when the sun doesn't shine or the wind doesn't blow strongly enough.

At the other end of the spectrum you have Big Tech. The world's major technology companies are much less carbon intensive and produce products that can support the clean energy transition—think of how video conferencing has reduced the need for corporate travel, or how electric cars are replacing the combustion engine. As a result, these firms are often rated highly for sustainability: some of the leaders are already deemed to be operating in line with the Paris Agreement's goal of limiting the global mean temperature rise to 1.5°C[40].

However, these companies own massive data centres, which consume huge amounts of electricity, much of which is still generated from fossil fuels, as well as vast amounts of water. The rise of AI compounds the issue. According to the Independent Energy Agency (IEA), a Paris-based autonomous intergovernmental organisation that provides advice and analysis on global energy issues, data centres and data transmission networks each account for 1–1.5% of global energy consumption, with AI expected to accelerate the growth in demand[41].

The sustainable investor's dilemma

This is not to say that either sector is wholly bad or good, but to highlight the difficulty of identifying truly sustainable investments. Investors therefore face a new dilemma: if you want your money to do more good than harm, *how* do you do it?

- Do you invest only in the few sectors that are truly sustainable, where companies are seeking to make a positive impact, but where the new technologies and solutions involved mean the risk is high?

- Or are you willing to back mainstream players who are making good progress on their transition and accept that, in the short term, the carbon intensity of your investments will be higher than you would like?

- If the latter, how do you balance your two objectives? Would you prefer to invest in a more sustainable company in a given sector or one which is performing better financially?

Finally, who is to make these judgements, and how? Investment managers now look at the sustainability characteristics of their investments along with the financial opportunities and risks – indeed, as we'll see, sometimes those sustainability characteristics create opportunities and risks – but it's not an exact science.

Some companies may be making good progress on their sustainability goals, while others might not. Some may disclose detailed analysis of their carbon footprint and sustainability progress while others might not. Analysts researching the companies factor all this in, but it's another layer of complexity.

In addition, an increasing number of investment managers see it as part of their role to be active participants in the company's sustainability strategy, often pushing company boards to make faster progress. Others take an entirely passive approach.

Navigating the complexity

The term 'greenwashing' was coined by environmentalist Jay Westerveld back in 1986. On a trip to Fiji, Westerveld noticed a sign in a hotel bathroom asking guests to reuse their towels to help the environment, but at the same time he observed that the resort was expanding with little regard for the island's ecosystem. Of course, reusing towels is more eco-friendly than sending them to be washed every day, but it doesn't do the bottom line any harm either – and the signs created a misleading impression of the hotel's concern for the environment.

Today, greenwashing is used to describe any action taken to make companies, investment products or other products appear more sustainable than they really are.

However, industry groups and regulators, including the UK's Financial Conduct Authority (FCA), are working hard to make it easier to identify genuinely sustainable companies and investments, versus instances of greenwashing. Standards of disclosure and labelling are improving all the time, providing increasingly effective ways of measuring the sustainability of your investments. Financial advisers are regulated by the FCA and benefit from the latest guidance on the topic, as well as requirements for how to take your preferences into account.

In the rest of this chapter, we'll look at the sustainability issues you might want to discuss with your adviser when considering your investment choices.

Climate change: Where are we today and where are we heading?

George watches the news every evening, and it's clear to him we're living at a critical moment in history. A day no longer goes by without news from somewhere in the world of the devastating impact of climate change – whether that's flooding in the Somerset Levels, the cities of Spain or the subways of New York; wildfires in Yorkshire, Australia or the holiday destinations of southern Europe; or persistent drought contributing to mass migration from Africa and the Middle East.

At the same time, as Aisha knows, there's a huge amount of work underway to support the transition to more sustainable economies worldwide. It's creating a wave of innovation in green technologies, clean energy, materials reuse and more, with all the investment opportunities that implies.

The impact of climate change is with us now, and importantly it will be with you for the duration of your investment journey. As a result, whether you see it as a risk, an opportunity or an issue you'd prefer not to think about, it's something your adviser can't afford to ignore in your investments.

The latest report from the Intergovernmental Panel on Climate Change (IPCC) makes for stark reading from any perspective[42]. Viewed through an investment lens, the scale of the potential impact is undeniable. Approximately 3.3 to 3.6 billion people – more than two fifths of the world's population – live in places or situations that are highly vulnerable to climate change. Land and water ecosystems have already seen substantial damage, reducing food and water security. Climate and weather extremes are driving population displacement in Africa, Asia, North America and Central and South America.

The IPCC models various paths to net zero, reflecting the climate pledges currently in place versus those needed to limit warming to 1.5% or 2%. Under all these scenarios, the cumulative rise in emissions means global warming will continue to increase in the near term (until 2040) and the adverse effects we are already experiencing will continue to intensify.

On a more positive note, the IPCC also says there is sufficient capital in the world to mitigate the effects of climate change and support the transition to net zero. Where the money flows will determine the extent that temperatures rise.

How you choose to respond to the changing climate – whether you simply want to manage the risks to your investments, invest in the opportunities or help to fund the transition – is of course up to you. What's important is that you understand your options, can discuss them with your adviser and ensure that an issue that will have a significant impact on the investment landscape is reflected in your plan.

The risks to your investments

Broadly speaking, the risks posed to investments by climate change can be grouped into six categories. These risks apply globally and in all sectors of the economy, but some regions and sectors are more vulnerable than others.

1. Physical risks

The most immediately apparent risks to investments from rising temperatures are the direct physical effects of climate change on company performance. These might include damage to company property, injuries and illness in the workforce, or limitations on the business's production capacity as a result of disruptions in the supply of materials or parts.

Sustainability risks to your investments

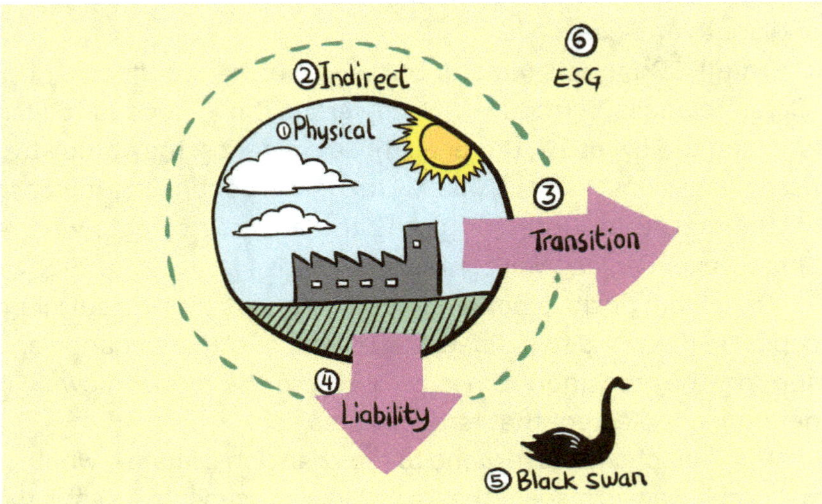

2. Indirect risks

These risks flow not directly from climate events or temperature increases but from their consequences. One example of an indirect climate effect might be forced mass migration and its impact on the political stability and economic conditions – and therefore the business environment – of the receiving country. Another is higher insurance costs as companies seek to protect themselves against direct risks.

3. Transition risks

Transition risks are the potential costs resulting from the shift to a low-carbon economy. One such risk is that of stranded assets – company assets that become worthless or are prematurely devalued because of the transition. Throughout the transition, many types of asset are likely to become obsolete as they are replaced with zero- or low-carbon alternatives. Other transition risks include the costs of complying with new regulations and adapting to technological change, as well as the potential reputational risk for companies that are slow to adjust.

4. Liability risks

Companies that don't adapt to the transition face another category of risk: the risk of fines and sanctions arising from failure to comply with new regulations and laws. Companies contributing to causing climate harm are also facing compensation claims from individuals, businesses or groups.

5. 'Black swan' risks

So called 'black swan' events are periods of high, complex and hard-to-predict risk in which many things go wrong at once. Climate change and other threats to our natural environment make such events more likely.

6. Other environmental, social and governance (ESG) risks

Together with governance issues related to the way companies are structured and managed, environmental and social considerations are referred to as ESG (environmental, social and governance) factors. Investment managers are increasingly expected to take these factors into account alongside traditional financial factors when choosing where to invest.

This chapter focuses on climate change as the biggest source of risk to our natural world. However, other environmental issues, such as use of water and other natural resources, use of plastics, and waste management, are increasingly affecting company bottom lines as consumer preferences and government regulations change.

Social issues such as inequality, workforce management and community relations are also gaining in importance for consumers and investors, and can create reputational and financial risks if not managed well.

The opportunities: a fourth industrial revolution

> **THE VALUE OF ADVICE**
> 'I have a client who's very positive about green energy. We were able to give him exposure to that in his portfolio, in line with his risk profile and without compromising his potential to achieve his financial goals.'

While climate change is a source of significant risk for investors, the global response is a huge area of opportunity. Reaching net zero requires wholesale changes to the way we live, work, eat and travel – and companies that successfully supply the sustainable alternatives to make these changes possible will thrive.

Climate change solutions are required in every sector, from more sustainable ways to feed growing populations to methods of decarbonising heavy industrial processes. Some of the technologies we will need for a low-carbon future are well-established, while others are at earlier stages. For investors, this creates a wide range of ways to play a role in the transition and share in the growth potential of innovative companies.

Beyond climate change, there are also increasing opportunities in biodiversity, water and waste management and other sustainability themes.

Investments in companies providing climate change solutions can be accessed through dedicated thematic funds. As with all new technologies, there will be winners and losers, so funds like this involve higher risk. Because she has a long time to ride out the ups and downs and is keen to use some of her money to support the transition, they might be something Aisha wants to think about as part of her overall portfolio.

Sustainability and performance: having your cake and eating it

THE VALUE OF ADVICE

'I have a client in her early 20s, a first time investor. She said to me, 'I wanted to be sustainable, but I didn't know how to invest in this way until we had our conversation about it.'

Is there a performance impact from investing sustainably? The short answer is: it depends on the approach. Historically, sustainable investment funds tended to exclude large parts of the market, which made it difficult to achieve market-level returns over time. Exclusions are still part of the toolkit for sustainable investors today, but many funds combine them with a more positive approach that focuses on companies with strong sustainability practices and actions towards transition.

One of the biggest academic studies of the impact of sustainable investing to date aggregated the findings of 2,000 smaller studies looking at the relationship between ESG factors and company performance. Over 90% of these studies found the relationship was either positive or neutral – meaning well-run companies that manage environmental and social factors tend to do at least as well as their peers if not better[43]. This makes sense if we think about the risks we've discussed above and their potential financial impact.

Companies with positive sustainability characteristics can be found in all sectors. Even in the most polluting sectors, such as energy and heavy industrials, some companies are playing an active role in the transition and are rapidly decarbonising, while others are being left behind.

George takes the view that investing in companies leading the transition in their sector rewards and incentivises progress. That position means it's possible for him to access the broad market, selecting companies with positive ESG characteristics across almost all sectors. As the study findings suggest, these funds have the potential to provide at least market-level returns, if not to outperform.

Takeaways

1. About two-thirds of advised investors place 'some' to 'very high' importance on the sustainability of their investments, while around a third see it of 'low' importance. Understanding your own preferences is important.
2. Investors wanting to do more good than harm with their money currently face a dilemma in choosing between investing in truly sustainable sectors, which often come with higher risks, or backing mainstream players making progress in their transition to sustainability.
3. Climate change poses significant risks to investments, including physical risks, transition risks and liability risks. These risks are global and affect all sectors of the economy. It's important that your investment solutions manage these risks.
4. The transition to a sustainable economy also presents significant investment opportunities in green technologies, clean energy and other innovative solutions.
5. Your adviser can help you understand where you sit on the issues discussed in this chapter, starting by understanding your sustainability profile.

8. Time-tested principles for investing

Sarah is new to investing and feels reassured by the idea of getting help from a financial adviser. She's used to keeping a tight rein on the family's money, though, so she wants to understand as much as possible about the decisions she and Stephen will make.

This chapter is for her – and for you if you feel the same. It's about all the choices that go into building the right investment plan for you: the types of investment you might hold, the globally accepted principles of sound investing, and how investments are packaged up into funds.

Stephen likes to find the right person for the job and let them get on with it. He doesn't need to know how the sausage is made. He might decide to skip this one, or just read the takeaways at the end.

Asset classes: the building blocks of your investment strategy

In chapter 5, we looked at a simple illustration of the main types of investment – often called 'asset classes' – available to you as an individual investor.

Let's look at the major ones in more detail.

Bonds

A bond is a loan made by an investor to a borrower, which might be a government or a company. The risk of a bond depends on who's borrowing the money. At one end of the spectrum, bonds called gilts are a way of lending money to the British government. The government stands behind the promise to pay, and as a result these bonds are seen as having no, or very low, risk.

You can also lend money to other developed market governments around the world, or to blue-chip companies (large, well-established and financially stable household names), which are perceived as more risky than governments but still fairly safe. Bonds from these issuers are known as investment grade bonds.

More risky still are bonds issued by companies with lower credit ratings, called high yield bonds, and bonds issued by governments and companies outside the developed world, called emerging market debt.

In return for the loan they receive, the bond issuer – the government or company borrowing the money – pays a defined level of regular interest, called a coupon, over a set period known as the term, or the life of the bond. At the end of that period, they must repay the amount borrowed.

The ability and willingness of bond issuers to keep paying their coupons and repay the loan at the end of the term is assessed by global credit rating agencies. The lower an issuer's credit rating and the higher the risk of the bond, the higher the coupon investors will want if they're going to buy the bond. The bond market is highly sophisticated, and you need a skilled manager to assess the trade-offs between risk and return.

Characteristics of bond investments

Income: Fixed

Because bonds pay a fixed coupon, the income you receive is steady and predictable.

Capital: Variable

If you bought a bond and held it throughout its term, you would get back the amount you invested at the end of that term – known as the principal repayment. In practice, though, bonds are often traded on the financial markets like other types of investment, and their value rises and falls according to factors such as interest rates and inflation expectations, perceptions of the issuer's creditworthiness, and levels of supply.

That means it's possible for the value of your bond investments to rise and to fall. However, bond prices – particularly for lower-risk bonds – tend to be less volatile (rise and fall less) than share prices.

Inflation protection: No

The coupons on bonds are set at the start of their term, with reference to interest rates at that time. Lots of factors influence coupon levels, but in simple terms, coupons for lower-risk bonds tend to be quite close to interest rates and those for higher-risk bonds quite a bit higher. When inflation increases, the buying power of those coupons falls.

Higher inflation also has an effect on bond prices. When inflation rises, interest rates usually rise too. The interest available from bank accounts will rise and newly issued bonds will have higher coupons. That makes bonds issued before inflation and interest rates rose look less appealing and their prices fall.

The main asset classes: risk vs. return

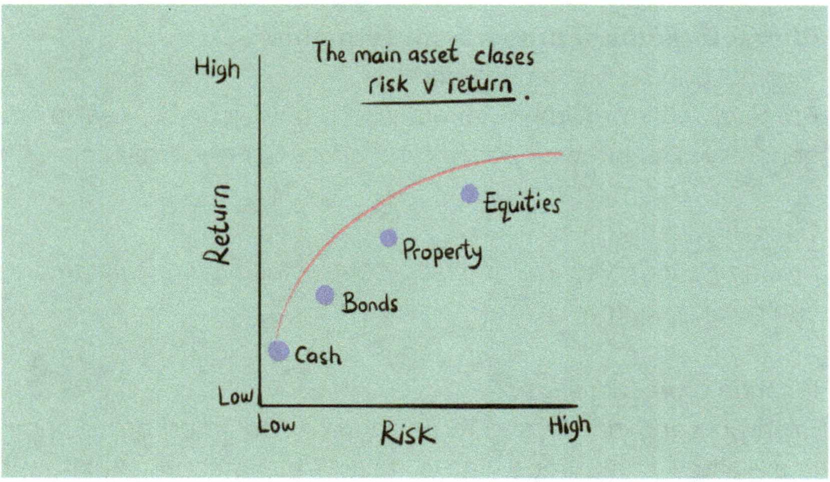

Property

As well as investing directly in bricks and mortar – in a second home, rental property or holiday let, for example – you can invest in property as part of your financial portfolio.

Property investments can be commercial property, such as office buildings, retail parks and warehouses, or in residential property. Some funds invest directly in property, but it's more common to gain exposure by investing in shares of property companies.

Property investments are more or less risky depending on the type and location of the property held. For example, an office building in a prime business district is likely to be rented out more consistently than one in a less sought-after part of the city, and so would be perceived as a less risky investment. Other factors such as the length of rental contracts also have an impact on the level of risk.

Property investments are affected by the fortunes of the economy and the property market, as well as by shifts in behaviours and preferences. For example, the rise of ecommerce has led to high demand for warehouse space, but weaker demand for physical retail space such as shopping centres. As a result, both prices and rents for warehouse space have risen, while prices and rents for retail space have fallen.

Characteristics of property investments

Income: Can be fixed or floating

Property rents provide investors with regular income. Leases are generally fixed but with periodic increases to reflect inflation.

Capital: Variable

Property prices also rise and fall, so the value of your investments can go up and down.

Inflation protection: Yes

Both property prices and rents tend to rise when other prices rise – albeit sometimes with a delay. That means investing in property can help to protect your money against the effects of inflation over the long term.

Shares or equities

As the name suggests, a share is simply a piece – your share – of a company. Also known as 'equities' and 'stocks', shares are issued by companies to raise money, with each share representing a certain proportion of the ownership. If the company is publicly listed, the shares can be bought and sold on stock markets.

As with other asset classes, some shares are riskier than others, but may offer higher rewards. In general, shares of developed market companies tend to be lower risk than those of emerging market companies, and shares of bigger, more established companies tend to be lower risk than those of smaller, faster-growing companies.

Share prices are affected by many factors, including the performance of the individual company, the sector or industry in which it does business, and the broader economy.

Characteristics of equity investments

Income: Variable

Some companies pay income in the form of dividends, which are distributions of profits to shareholders. Dividends are not fixed, and companies may reduce them or scrap them completely in challenging times.

Capital: Variable

Share prices rise and fall, so the value of your investments can go up and down.

Inflation protection: Maybe

When prices rise, costs for companies rise. Companies may be able to pass these increases on to their customers in the form of higher prices, protecting their profits – and the returns for their shareholders – from the effect of inflation. However, sometimes that doesn't work out: instead, customers respond by finding cheaper substitutes or cutting their spending.

The goods and/or services the company provides, whether they are essentials or luxuries, and the availability of substitutes all have an effect, as does the broader economic landscape. So some companies are better protected from inflation than others, and shares offer more protection in some environments than others.

Major asset classes at a glance

	Income	Capital	Inflation protection
Cash	Variable	Fixed	✗
Bonds	Fixed	Variable	✗
Property	Fixed/Variable	Variable	✓
Shares	Variable	Variable	?

Private assets: as well as the major asset classes above, you might also have heard about private assets. These are investments that aren't traded on public markets such as stock exchanges. Instead, they're bought, sold and held privately. They used to be the preserve of large institutions such as pension funds and insurance companies, but they're becoming more accessible to individual investors.

Private equity is investment in companies not listed on the stock market.

Private credit is a way of lending money to companies directly, as opposed to by buying their bonds.

Infrastructure investments finance essential assets such as public transport networks, power grids and water systems.

Your adviser can talk to you about whether these asset classes are suitable for you and how you could use them in your portfolio.

Why do asset classes matter?

The asset classes you invest in matter because they're the most important driver of the risk you take and the return you get. Many studies show this, with the most well-known being by Brinson, Hood and Beebower[44]. The authors found that investors' asset allocation over the long term was the biggest cause of variation in their returns (more than 90% of the difference in returns). That means, for example, that the proportion of shares to bonds in a portfolio had much more effect on the return achieved than the specific shares and bonds the investors held.

Today, asset allocation is a central part of the task for advisers and investment managers. Looking at your risk profile and objectives, along with your other preferences, they assess which combination of asset classes is most likely to produce the greatest return for the risk you are willing and able to take.

Drivers of portfolio performance

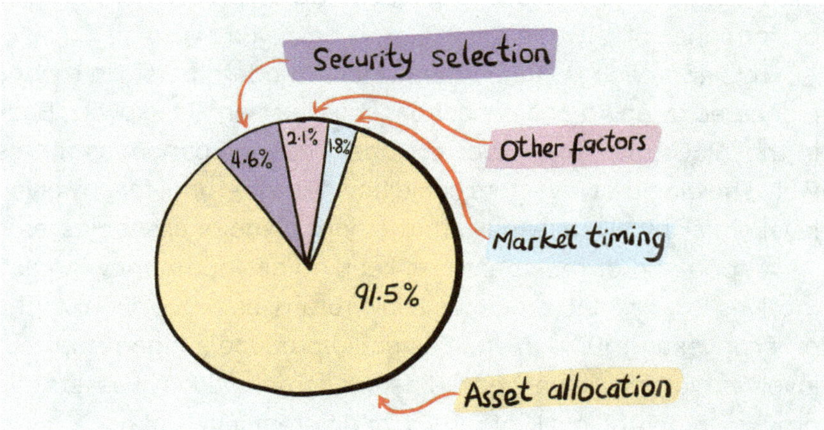

Diversification: the cornerstone of investing

> **THE VALUE OF ADVICE**
>
> 'In the late 90s, a client was riding the crest of a wave with his self-invested share portfolio. Each time we met, he'd show me how much better his investments were doing compared to the "sluggish" returns of the diversified pension we looked after. When the tech bubble burst, the value of his investments collapsed by more than 80%. Thereafter, he handed everything over to us. He's now semi-retired and in a very comfortable position.'

The largest institutions around the world follow a set of widely agreed, time-tested principles when investing their money – and today they've become best practice for individual investors too.

- **First**, determine your desired level of risk.
- **Then** find the right blend of asset classes to be invested in.
- **Then** find the right investments within those asset classes.

Underpinning these principles is the idea of not putting all your eggs in one basket, more formally known as 'diversification': spreading out your money across a wide range of investments, markets, sectors and asset classes, rather than relying on the performance of any one.

This approach is the cornerstone of modern portfolio theory, pioneered by an American economist called Harry Markowitz. Back in the 1950s, Markowitz won a Nobel Prize in Economics for his work showing that investors could boost their returns for any given level of risk by diversifying with the right blend of asset classes[45].

At one end of the spectrum, keeping all your money in cash involves low risk and produces a low return, as we've seen. At the other, investing 100% in equities could produce a high return but involves high risk. In between, different combinations of assets can produce different levels of return for different levels of risk.

Diversification works because different asset classes tend to behave in different ways at different parts of the economic cycle. In the illustration below, asset class A tends to rise at certain times (for example, when the economy is growing), while asset class B tends to fall at those times. When the economy is contracting or in recession, asset class B tends to do better.

Imagine, then if you constructed a portfolio (line C) made up of half asset class A (for example, equities) and half asset class B (for example, bonds). The portfolio would deliver a return that was the average of both classes – and, more importantly, it would be less risky: it would move up and down a lot less than being 100% invested in either asset class.

Illustrative relationship between two asset classes, A and B

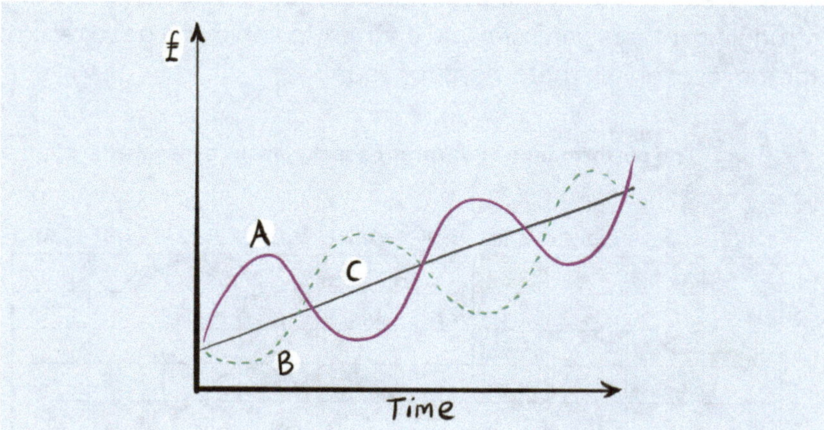

In practice, the relationships between different asset classes – known as correlations – don't tend to be stable. However, they can be estimated over the long term. Understanding correlations has proven to be very valuable in identifying the combination of assets that deliver an optimal level of return for a given risk level.

Which asset classes will perform the best?

If asset classes are the biggest driver of investment returns, surely the most sensible thing to do would be to pick the class that delivers the highest return and stick with it? Ah, would that it were so simple! Another reason that diversification is important is that it's rare for the same asset class to perform best each year.

The illustration below shows the performance of different asset classes over the last decade[46]. Each colour represents a different asset class – but don't worry about deciphering them all. Instead, focus on UK equity (the dark brown boxes). In 2018 and 2020, it was at the bottom – the worst performing asset class for the year. In 2022, it was at the top. In other years, it was somewhere in between.

Pick any other colour and you're likely to see something similar: some good years, some mediocre, and some bad. Can any of us predict which will do best next year? Unlikely.

Instead of trying to forecast the winner, a better approach is to invest in a range of asset classes, so that when some are struggling, others can keep you on track to achieving good returns for the level of risk that's right for you.

The performance of different asset classes over time

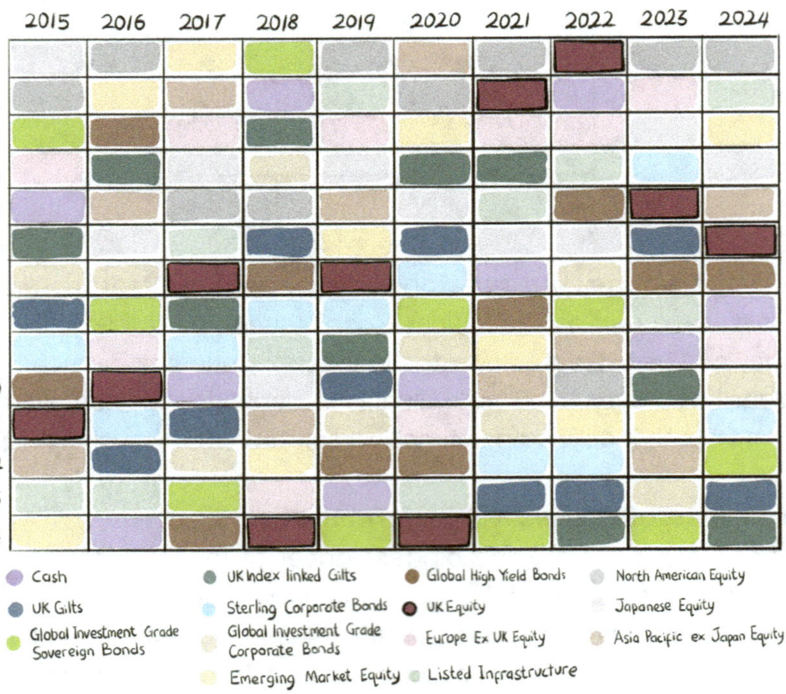

Over time, the understanding of asset classes and their potential returns, risk and correlation with other classes has become more and more granular. Advisers and investment managers might consider dozens of asset classes, with equities, for example, broken down by region and then by company size (known as market capitalisation, or market cap). As a result, there are more ways to build you a diversified portfolio designed to maximise your return for the level of risk you're willing and able to take.

Today, asset classes are understood at a more granular level

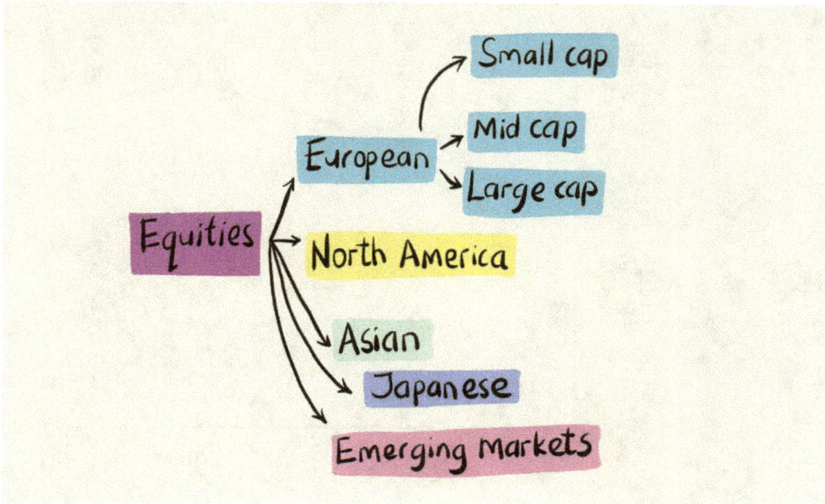

We've also learned that correlations can break down completely in extreme periods. We now know it's important to use a way of modelling risk that looks forwards as well as backwards to factor in these extremes. However, the principle Markowitz established – and the globally established best practices for investing – remains the same.

Markowitz showed there's an optimum combination for each risk level. He called this 'the efficient frontier': the optimal composition of your portfolio, based on the level of risk you want to take. He found that a diversified portfolio delivers higher returns for a given level of risk than investing in any single asset class alone. This understanding is good news for investors because it can help to prevent you from taking more risk than you need to for the return you want to achieve.

To put all of this into action, your adviser will work with you to understand the level of risk that's right for you and then translate that into an investment strategy. Their chosen investment manager or managers will use that strategy to deliver the best return they can for you at that given level of risk, starting at the asset class level and then looking at how best to get exposure to that asset class.

The benefits of diversification[47]

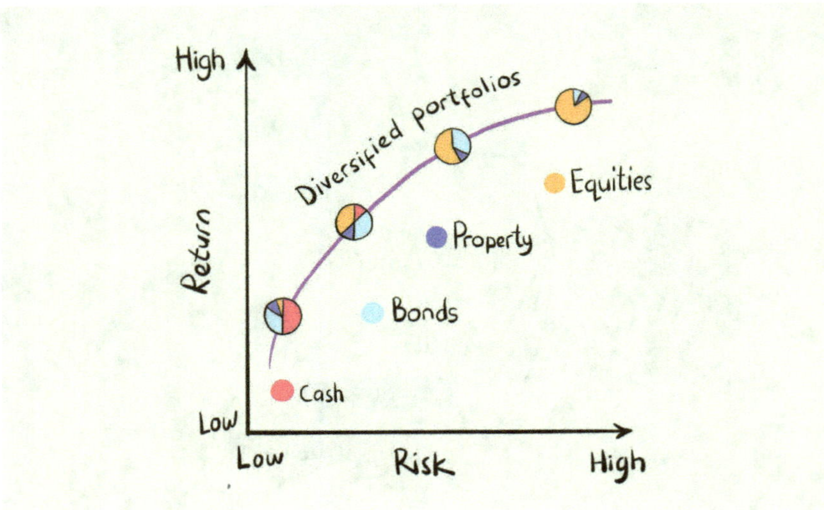

Types of investing

> **THE VALUE OF ADVICE**
> 'Often, clients who move to us after managing their own investments are no longer enjoying it. It's either taking too much time and worry or they have made no changes and not reviewed anything at all since the investments started.'

Investing through funds

Over the years, George has dabbled in the stock market himself. Although he's finding it harder to keep track these days, in the past he liked to pick up stock tips from the papers and make small investments. He saw them as more of a flutter, alongside his sensible private pension and savings – which was a good job, because they didn't always pay off.

When you invest as an individual through a financial adviser, the most common way to access investments such as shares, bonds and property is through funds or managed portfolios. Your money is pooled with the money of other investors, and a professional fund manager invests on behalf of all of you. This way of investing enables you to diversify your money more widely, rather than making only a handful of investments – so it matters much less if some of your individual holdings do badly.

The most common types of fund are mutual funds (in the UK, often called Open-Ended Investment Companies) and exchange-traded funds, or ETFs. The main difference between these is the way they are bought and sold. Mutual funds are bought directly from investment companies, while ETFs are traded on stock exchanges, like shares.

Active and passive investing

Another choice is whether you want to use active funds, passive funds or a combination of the two. What's the difference?

In active approaches, investment managers use research to try to predict which specific investments or asset classes will do better than the overall market (outperform) and which will do worse (underperform). They invest more in the investments they think will do well and less in those they think will do badly, trying to give you a return that's higher than that of the overall market.

In passive investing, managers instead try to replicate a market or asset class – say, the UK stock market – as closely as possible, holding the same shares in the same proportions as an index of that market, such as the FTSE 100. The fees tend to be cheaper than for active management, but you don't have the opportunity to do better than the market.

Some investors choose active investing because they feel comforted by the knowledge that there's an expert looking at their money day in, day out, trying to add value on their behalf and putting the brakes on when the market gets too choppy. Others are happy to ride out the peaks and troughs of the market, getting the average market return. It's really up to you.

Multi-asset investing

Today, it's very common for investment managers to combine different asset classes, including shares, bonds, property, cash and perhaps others, in single funds or portfolios. This is called multi-asset investing.

Some multi-asset funds have static allocations – for example, 50% equities, 40% bonds, 10% cash. Others shift their allocations actively as market and economic conditions change, with the aim of achieving higher returns and managing risk.

Returns versus income

As we saw above, some asset classes produce income – such as coupons from bonds, rental income from property or dividends from shares. How you use this income – and how you balance income and returns – depends on your needs and where you are on your investment journey.

If you're saving for retirement, like Aisha, and you don't currently need income from your investments, your adviser will prioritise returns (capital growth) over income. Any income your investments provide can be reinvested. Because that reinvested income will then benefit from compounding, it can be a significant source of return over time.

Once you're in retirement, like George, you might need to take the income from your investments. Depending on any other sources of income available to you and the amount of money you've built up for retirement, you might also still need to generate returns. We'll look in more detail at balancing the two later.

As with your capital, your income can be exposed to lower or higher risk. For example, coupons from gilts are highly stable and predictable, whereas dividends from shares can fluctuate significantly. Different types of income are also treated differently for tax purposes – again, this is something your adviser can help you to optimise.

Time in the market, not timing the market

As we said at the start, this is a book for people who expect to achieve their goals over the longer term. A key ingredient of that approach is time. We've seen how the wonder of compounding turns small returns into large ones over the years. Your job is to leave it to do that work.

In economic downturns, or when the headlines are shouting about falling markets, it can be tempting to take your money out. It might feel safer to stay on the shore for a while and plan to go back in when the water's calmer. But getting the timing right is notoriously difficult – and many of the best days for markets come immediately after heavy falls. Missing just the start of the recovery can have a huge impact on your returns over time.

To illustrate that, let's look at the returns you would have gained if you had taken a medium level of risk (risk level 5) since Dynamic Planner started formally measuring these through an index, a period of just over 13 years[48].

Staying invested matters

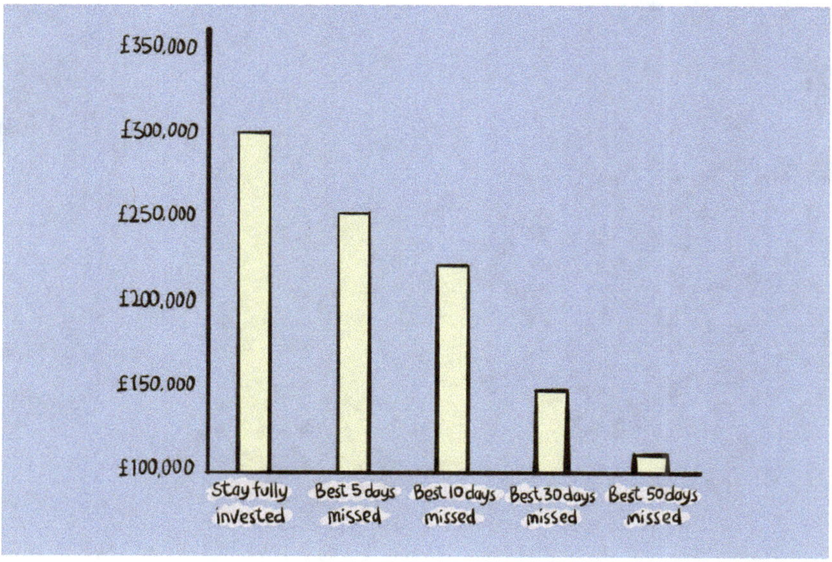

If you'd invested £100,000 at the start of the period and remained invested throughout, you'd now have £300,000. But if you'd gone in and out of the market, the picture would look quite different.

If you'd missed just the best five days on the market, you'd end the period with around £250,000. If you'd missed the best ten, you'd have around £220,000. Missed the best 30? You've now got less than £150,000.

The message? When times are tough, sit on your hands. Over the long term, markets have always recovered. Once you've got your risk profile right, you can afford to ride out the ups and downs. Long experience shows that, hands down, time in the market beats trying to time the market.

This has been a whistlestop tour of the basic concepts of investing. It should provide a strong foundation for you to have good conversations with your adviser, and to think about questions you might want to ask.

Takeaways

1. Once you've identified the right level of risk, the next important decision is which asset classes you should invest in. Asset classes are responsible for the majority of the difference in returns people achieve. The selection of individual investments has a much smaller effect.
2. Diversification across multiple asset classes and investments is a globally tried-and-tested way to maximise the level of return you get for a given level of risk.
3. Done well, diversification goes beyond 'not keeping all your eggs in one basket', and will actually boost your returns.
4. There are different types of investing: via funds or portfolios, active or passive, as income or growth focused. These are all choices you can discuss with your adviser.
5. Time invested in the market is the important thing. Trying to time the market – buying and selling to catch a bounce – is a high-risk strategy that rarely pays off.

9. Identifying your investment profiles

As we've seen, Sarah feels very uncertain about risking her hard-earned money by investing it. With the help of a financial adviser, and with time and experience, we know statistically that her confidence is likely to grow – but not if her experience of investing keeps her awake at night.

Stephen has run a business for years and got very used to weighing up risk and reward. His priority is to complete the shift to charity work as soon as he can – and if more risk can make that happen faster, he's happy with it.

George is a seasoned investor and comfortable with taking some risk with his money. If he's leaving more of it in the bank these days, it's only because he's started to find researching investments a chore. But he might lose sleep if he feels the returns he is getting on his investments come at the expense of his grandchildren's future.

The happiness this book aims to help you achieve is not a pot of gold at the end of the rainbow. It's not about being happy *one day* – importantly, not at the expense of your happiness now.

Although there are often trade-offs when it comes to financial planning, the ideal is to find a way to fund a future happiness that you're comfortable with in the present as well. That's why your adviser will want to really understand how you feel about investing before they start to work on building your plan.

To do this they will ask you a series of questions through one or more questionnaires. These are quick and simple to answer but are designed to get under the skin of how you actually feel about some of the topics we've looked at, such as risk and sustainability.

Areas covered might include:

- Investment experience
- Attitude to risk
- Capacity to take risk
- Selecting your risk profile
- Sustainability
- Wellness and any vulnerabilities you may have
- Your income needs in retirement (where applicable)

Understanding your investment experience

Are you a first-time investor? Is your experience limited to paying into a pension at work or – at the other end of the spectrum – do you have a wide range of investments, some or all of which you look after yourself? Your adviser will want to know this information because there's a link between your level of experience, knowledge and the types of investment you're likely to be confident and comfortable with.

They will also be interested in how often you like to engage with your investments – regularly or irregularly – and how you have historically reacted if the value of your investments has fluctuated substantially. All of this helps build up a profile of your experience and confidence.

Your attitude to risk

We've seen that our attitudes to risk – in general and when it comes to our finances – have many influences: our DNA, our experiences in childhood and in later life, our parents' attitudes, their own childhood experiences, our friendships and social circle. The effect of these factors is not predictable: one person who's lived through tough economic times might become very risk averse, while another might come to embrace risk.

Your attitude to risk is not dissimilar to whether you're naturally more introverted or extraverted, or whether you tend to seek new experiences or prefer to stay with what you know[49]. There's no right or wrong answer, and these influences tend to run deep. As a result, they drive both our happiness and our desire to act under certain circumstances. It's for this reason that understanding your attitude to risk is a vital part of building your plan. One person's comfortable level of ups and downs (Stephen's, for example) is another's sleepless nights (Sarah's) – and sleepless nights are no one's idea of happiness.

Your adviser will help you think about your willingness to take risk – often called your risk appetite. As part of this process, they will ask you to complete a questionnaire in which you answer questions about your attitude to risk.

Dynamic Planner's version of this – the most widely used in the country, used to profile over 2 million people to date – is what's known as a psychometric questionnaire. This approach to determining your attitude to risk doesn't rely on your self-knowledge – because knowing yourself can be difficult. Instead, it uses scientific methods and questions that are very easy to answer to assess your attitude to risk. While there are definitely no right or wrong answers, the questionnaire is also designed to uncover any areas worth a discussion between you and your adviser – perhaps areas where you're pulled in two directions at once.

The test looks at different components that together drive how you feel about taking risk:

- **Risk-taking identity**: Your self-identity is your perception of the kind of person you are. Perhaps you tend to see yourself as strong, as funny or as kind. Your identity is composed of both personal elements and elements that relate to the social groups and cultures you belong to. There's strong evidence to suggest we're driven to behave in ways that reflect our self-identity – so if you see yourself as a risk-taker (Stephen does; Sarah doesn't), you're more likely to be willing to take risks.

- **Fear of missing out (FOMO)**: You might be familiar with FOMO as something that makes people go to parties when they'd rather stay at home on the sofa. But its influence on our choices goes far beyond that. FOMO is used by advertisers to make us believe we're missing opportunities others are not, and it can also influence our investment decisions. This is particularly apparent when the value of an asset increases dramatically over a short period of time – and is one reason why otherwise sensible people are frequently burnt by getting involved in investments that shoot up in value only to collapse later on.

- **Preference for certainty**: Remember the coin-toss experiment back in chapter 3? Kahneman and Tversky found that the prospect of a loss looms much larger for people than the potential for gains. The same researchers also showed that people place outsize importance on certainty and therefore prefer certain gains over larger gains that involve risk.

- **Uncertainty tolerance**: People who are intolerant of uncertainty feel anxious in situations where it's not clear what will happen in the future, so tend to avoid those situations. Sarah has been at the same school throughout her teaching career, for example, though she might have progressed more quickly if she'd moved. Those with this trait are much less likely than others to make investments that involve risk or participate in the stock market.

- **Emotions towards investing**: A large body of research exploring emotions and financial decisions shows those in positive emotional states of any kind tend to be more likely to take risk. Negative emotional states, though, have different effects. Fear makes people risk-avoidant, whereas anger can cause people to feel more confident in their abilities and therefore to take bigger, more reckless risks.

The test aims to uncover where you sit in relation to each of these factors. The output is a description of how you feel about risk, which you can read and discuss with your adviser. Does it feel true? Is there anything you disagree with?

The test isn't a one-and-done. Your risk attitude can and, likely will, change over time. As people gain more experience of taking investment risk, their appetite tends to increase. Then, as they move into their later years, it tends to decrease. These are averages, though, and you are an individual, so your adviser may well ask you to complete an attitude-to-risk questionnaire every year or two to check if anything has changed.

Your capacity to take risk

The final part of your risk profile is how much risk you can afford to take. This is determined by the amount of money you have available to invest, the level of resources you have (income, other assets etc) outside of this investment, your financial commitments, and where you are in your investment journey in relation to your goals.

Think back to the work you did on life phases in chapter 4. If, like George, you're in later life, retired and living off the income from some of the money you've saved, you may need to avoid large ups and downs in the value of your investments. If, like Aisha, you're investing early in your career, you've got lots of time ahead of you to ride out the bumps, so can afford to take more risk.

Your adviser will look at your circumstances with you to work out this aspect of your profile. It's also important they understand what's important to you and are aware of what you must do, versus what you'd like to do and what you dream of. That way you can work out together how to make sure your essential expenses and goals aren't compromised by taking risk.

Selecting your risk profile

> **THE VALUE OF ADVICE**
>
> 'I had a client who wasn't that interested in the process and thought he knew what he wanted to invest in. It was only when he saw the example asset allocation for that risk profile that he said, "That amount in shares? No, that's too much for me. It's about taking the time and using different ways of communicating to make sure the client understands and is comfortable with the risk they're taking on.'

Your adviser will work with you to find the optimal balance of your investment experience, your attitude to risk and your capacity to take it, along with your objectives for your money. This is your risk profile. It's usually expressed on a scale: the Dynamic Planner version uses a scale from one (lowest / most risk averse) to ten (highest/most risk tolerant), but different firms might use different names or categories.

Together, you will discuss the implications of your risk profile. The best way of doing it is with an asset allocation that aligns with your profile – because, as we saw in chapter 8, the asset classes you invest in are the biggest determinant of your risk and return. It's only an example and not your final portfolio, but it will help you understand the range of potential gains and losses you might experience in the future, how bumpy the journey might be, and how this profile has performed historically versus the alternatives. If it works for you: great; if not, your risk profile can be adjusted as needed.

In other words, the output of the risk profiling process is a starting point, not the whole story. You can work with your adviser and look at different profiles until you're happy.

A note on investing as a couple

If you and your partner are making financial plans together, you should ideally complete the risk assessment process separately. You may find you have different attitudes to risk. If so, it's good to acknowledge these before working with your adviser to find a balance between you. Some couples choose to invest separately so they're both comfortable, while others find a compromise.

In Stephen and Sarah's case, Stephen's attitude to risk is a high medium (7 out of 10) whereas Sarah's is a low medium (4 out of 10). After some discussion with their new adviser, they decide to build a plan to invest together, at a medium risk (5 out of 10). Sarah accepts taking slightly high risk with their investments to get them where they want to go faster, and Stephen slightly less so that Sarah is comfortable.

Agreeing your sustainability profile

Like George, you might be keen to invest in a way that benefits the planet, or at least that does less harm – but how important is it to you in comparison with your financial goals? This can be difficult to quantify.

As with risk profiling, psychometric testing can help you find the right balance. Although this is a newer field, there has been lots of academic work to determine the factors that contribute to people's sustainability preferences when investing[50].

Factors assessed in a psychometric sustainability test include:

- **Psychological distance:** People tend to take more risks with decisions that are further away in time. When we apply this to climate change, we can see that acting now might be unattractive for some people because the promise of reward feels both distant and uncertain. Social and geographical distance also have an impact – people are more motivated to make decisions that benefit people to whom they are emotionally and physically close rather than, for example, future generations or those on the other side of the world. A measure of psychological distance explores how you perceive the impact of investing sustainably on the present and future, on yourself and others.

- **Personal values:** In the past, your adviser might have assumed your sole goal was to maximise your wealth. However, some investors are also motivated to contribute to environmental or social change, meaning they want to seek investments that are consistent with their values and are willing to accept lower returns if necessary. Investing sustainably, like making environmentally conscious consumer decisions, can also be a way for people to define themselves, or express to their peers what matters to them.

- **Emotional benefit:** Research shows that investing sustainably can also provide a feelgood factor: investors benefit emotionally when it's demonstrated that they've acted responsibly with their investment decisions, and can even feel compensated by this social benefit if they are told they may receive lower returns. Assessing your emotions about how companies manage environmental and social risks – for example, how much it matters to you that companies share your values – is therefore an important part of a sustainability profile.

- **Positive impact:** Some people not only want to avoid harm or manage environmental and social risks but want to make a positive difference with their money. Questions on this topic are designed to assess the extent to which this is a priority.

- **Financial considerations:** Studies show that investments with positive environmental, social and governance (ESG) characteristics can perform at least as well as traditional investments. The broad range of sustainable investing solutions available today means that for most people there isn't the trade-off between sustainability and returns that there was in the past. However, it's still important to understand how you prioritise your opportunities and returns versus your sustainability preferences.

Your sustainability profile may be expressed as a number or in terms of the importance you place on the topic – from 'low' to 'very high'.

Regardless of where you fit in, if you work with an adviser to find the right balance of risk and return, there will be a broad range of solutions available to you in 97% of cases. If you're in the 3% of people with a very strong preference to deliver a positive impact with their money, you may need specialist advice.

Assessing your financial wellbeing

The financial services regulator, the Financial Conduct Authority (FCA), wants advisers to assess whether their clients have characteristics that make them financially vulnerable – meaning they are more likely to fall into a state of hardship that would make it difficult for them to maintain their standard of living.

All of us are at risk of becoming vulnerable, but the FCA has identified four drivers that increase the risk. Your adviser will want to assess whether they apply to you either through a discussion or using a wellbeing questionnaire.

- **Health:** Health conditions or illnesses that affect your ability to carry out day-to-day tasks.

- **Life events:** Events such as bereavement, job loss or relationship breakdown.

- **Resilience:** Low ability to withstand financial or emotional shocks.

- **Capability:** Low understanding of financial matters or low confidence in your ability to manage your money.

This assessment touches on matters that are quite personal, but it's valuable for you and your adviser – and remember, advisers are very used to these conversations and you're unlikely to say anything they haven't heard before. All of us have periods in life when we're more financially vulnerable, such as after the death of a partner. The aim of a wellbeing questionnaire is simply to make sure your adviser can provide the support you need and communicate with you in the ways that best suit you.

Identifying your retirement income preferences

If, like George, you're at a time in your life when receiving an income from your investments is a priority – or is likely to become one soon – then understanding your needs and preferences for that income is another important part of your profile.

This is an area that you and your adviser should explore carefully due to the need to balance seven areas: the certainty, accessibility, consistency and flexibility of your income, your need for inflation proofing, your need or desire for a lump sum at the point of retirement or after, and your desire to leave a legacy. Very few people can get all of these, so you'll probably need to make some trade-offs.

The income balancing act

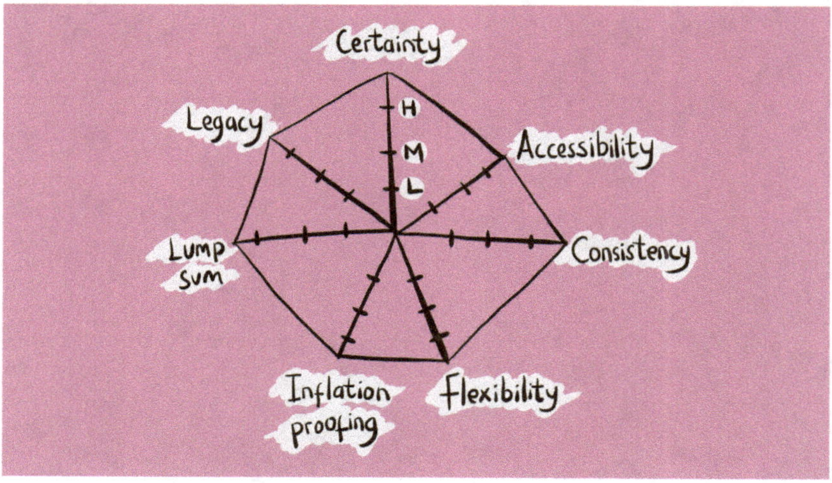

George, for example, is already retired and has no big purchases on the horizon, so he doesn't need a lump sum. He's in the habit of planning his spending carefully, and it doesn't change a lot from year to year, so certainty matters more to him than flexibility. He is thinking about his legacy though, and he'd like something left at the end to give his grandkids a good start in life.

You might share his priorities, or yours might be very different. Your adviser will help you identify what matters to you, and may use a questionnaire to help you get the right balance.

Next steps

You know where you're starting from. You know where you want to get to. You know how you feel about the journey and how much risk you want to take along the way.

With all that in place, it's time to start building your plan. The bulk of the work sits with your adviser, but they should discuss it with you every step of the way and make adjustments as necessary until you feel comfortable that you're on a path to happiness. In the next chapters, we'll look at what goes into that process.

Takeaways

1. Your adviser will want to understand how you feel about investing before they start work building your plan or recommending solutions. To do this, they'll ask you to complete one or more questionnaires. If you're planning as a couple, you should do these separately and then go through them with your adviser together.
2. Your risk profile is a function of three things: your level of investment experience; your attitude to risk, influenced by factors such as personality and past experiences; and your capacity to take risk, based on your resources, commitments, financial goals and life stage.
3. A sustainability questionnaire helps your adviser to understand the importance you place on factors such as the environmental and social impact of your investments, and how to balance that with your financial goals.
4. Assessing your financial wellbeing, or how vulnerable you are to falling into a state of financial hardship, is key to making sure you're getting the support you need.
5. If you're in or near retirement, your income needs and preferences should be carefully balanced to find the right solution for you – for example, is it more important to you to know exactly what you'll get each month or to have some flexibility about the money you have available to spend? Again, a questionnaire can help.

10. Building your plan: vision and resources

Once you've agreed your profiles, you and your adviser are ready to build your financial plan.

Like any good plan, you should begin with the end in mind.

Before they had their children, Stephen and Sarah travelled together all over the world. They got huge amounts of satisfaction from planning a trip, evaluating the different routes and potential places to stay, thinking through the timings and costs – and then, having decided on the best approach, seeing those plans come to fruition. That feeling of accomplishment – of having figured something out and then successfully acted on it – is what this chapter is all about.

It will bring together many of the topics we've covered in previous chapters so you feel prepared to discuss and agree with your adviser the best route forward. And so you're on track to fund the life you want to live – to fund your happiness and that of those who depend on you financially.

Beginning with the end in mind

In chapter 4 you defined your vision of happiness – the things you must, would like to and dream of funding, and the different phases of your life when you'd like them to happen. You can see it all before you.

Perhaps, like Stephen and Sarah, that might be a financially secure retirement, with the time and resources to travel and focus on charity work. Perhaps, like Aisha, it's leaving the corporate world and going out on your own so you can spend more time with your children. Maybe, like George, you're thinking about making gifts to the next generation. Or maybe you have other ideas and dreams.

A plan to find happiness

Your adviser can help you to make your ideas even more concrete by:

- Discussing landmarks along the way, such as paying down debts, funding holidays, getting a promotion or selling a business.
- Identifying potential challenges and choices, and your preferred routes given the terrain.
- Working out what's feasible given the risks you are willing and able to take and your preferences for investing sustainably.

This conversation about future goals and happiness will almost certainly take a little time and may need more than a single session. Once the destination and milestones are set, it's the job of your adviser to come up with a route map for you and to look at the art of the possible – the potential routes from where you are today to those future destinations.

In financial planning, this route map is known as your 'cash flow plan'. It's a document, typically digital, to help you check in with progress over time, adjusting your course where needed, to help you fund the life you want to live.

This chapter explains two key pieces of the cash flow plan:

1. **Where are you today?**

    a. What resources (incomes, investments, properties, business interests) do you have, or could you have in the future, and when?

    b. What obligations (expenses, debts, mortgages) do you have today, or might you have in the future?

2. **Are your existing investments (if you have any) a good match for your profile?** How much risk are you taking, how are they performing given that risk and are you paying any unnecessary costs?

Where are you today?

> **THE VALUE OF ADVICE**
>
> 'My favourite story is when a comfortable retirement looked touch and go for a couple I worked with. I was going through the biscuit tin with them to find everything I could and the guy pulled out a tatty old brown Army Pension book. I did a rough calculation and then went away and checked it out properly and it was a few grand a year. They were so happy and couldn't quite believe it.'

The starting point for your plan is your current situation, resources and arrangements. In chapter 4, you completed a list of your current incomes and outgoings, including how and when you expect these to start and finish, rise or fall during your life phases. The more you can flesh this out, the more useful it will be.

If, like Aisha, you're earlier in your journey, it's likely your arrangements are simpler, that you have less accumulated savings and investments, and more debt.

In mid-life, like Stephen and Sarah, we tend to have more put away, perhaps one or more pensions, some existing investments, bank savings and equity in your home or business. You might have credit cards, a mortgage or other debts to service as well. If you have a family, there will be other costs to factor in – perhaps school or educational costs to fund. You may have some long-term insurance in place such as life insurance or critical illness cover, as well the insurance you need for daily life, like car, home and pet insurance.

In later life, like George, the picture can become more complex still, with a working lifetime of financial arrangements behind you, including, perhaps, a will.

Let's look in more detail at all the pieces of the puzzle to help you and your adviser build up a complete picture of what you own and what you owe. At the end of this section, you'll find a checklist to help you pull everything together and make sure you don't miss anything.

Where am I today?

Savings, investments and pensions

Where is your money at the moment and how much is in each place? Think about bank savings accounts, ISAs, workplace and personal pensions, investment accounts and any other types of investment you hold.

Are you paying into these accounts and investments today and, if so, how much? Is anyone else contributing – for example, is your employer making pension contributions? Can your money be accessed immediately or is it locked away for a certain period? Do any other benefits come with your savings – for example, older savings policies may have some form of life insurance associated with them? Do you expect to receive income or lump sums – for example, pay rises, bonuses, interest, dividends, inheritances or proceeds from the sale of property or a business?

To understand the risk you're *currently* taking (this may be different from the risk you *plan* to take), your adviser will want to know about your investments and where they are held. They'll use tools to look under the bonnet at your underlying investments (for example, the shares held in a fund), as these are important components of the risk you're taking. Your adviser can also assess whether you're making use of the tax efficiencies available to you and whether you're holding any unregulated investments that expose you to outsized risks.

Property

If you're a homeowner this includes your home, but also any other properties you own – perhaps a second home or rental properties. Do you own these properties outright or do you have mortgages on them? The cost of debt, the timing to repay it and the type of mortgage are all considerations in a good financial plan. If you have equity in your home (that is, if your home is worth more than any mortgage on it), it's an asset that can contribute to your overall plan.

Aisha succeeds in buying a two-bedroom house with the help of a repayment mortgage. She takes this out with a deposit of £21,000, which she is able to put down through her own savings and some help from her parents. She got a good fixed-rate deal when she bought the house and that makes her payments manageable. That said, she has half an eye on the end of the fixed term in 18 months' time, and her adviser will want to factor that into their cash flow planning.

Typically, you would expect to benefit from growth in value of your house over the long run. The value of your mortgage will stay static, assuming you pay off your interest, or fall if you have a repayment mortgage. Over time, that means your equity would normally be expected to grow too. Of course, it's not always the case – house prices can fall in value as well as rise, and these falls can be made worse by the impact of inflation. The oil crisis in the 1970s, recession in the early 1990s, the global financial crisis of 2008 and the post-Covid slump of 2022 all negatively affected house prices[51].

Nevertheless, for Aisha, being on the property ladder feels like a good thing – in terms both of providing a home for her and Sammy and of reasonably being able to expect that her property will increase in value over time.

Long-term data shows house prices fall as well as rise

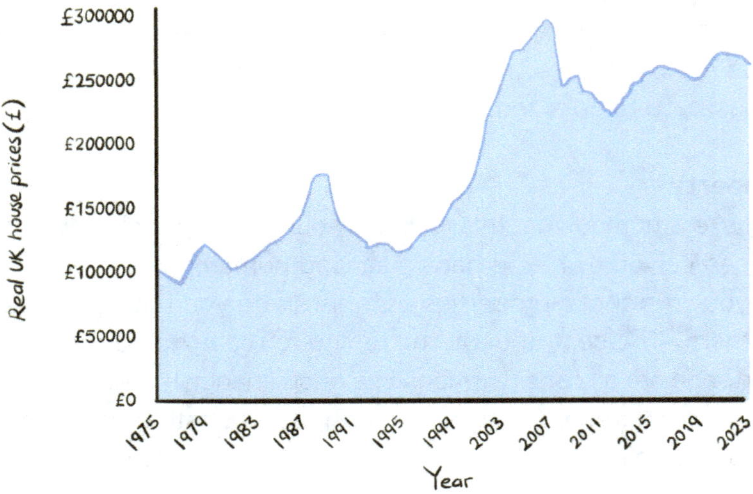

The average annual growth rate for property in the UK over the last 30 years has been around 5–6% before accounting for the effects of inflation – a long-term return similar to a low to medium-risk investment. This level of return does vary significantly around the country and is dependent on the type of house, its condition and so on. But if you consider that you don't pay capital gains tax on the sale of your own home as long as you live there, it makes sense for Aisha to have prioritised home ownership, as long as she can continue to afford the repayments and is prepared to weather any storms should prices drop at a time she might want to sell.

George is at the other end of his property journey. He is mortgage free, having paid off his loan some years ago and benefited from the really rapid rise in properly prices in the 1990s. His detached four-bed property with a nice garden, which he bought in the village for £160,000 in 1980, is now worth between £375,000 and £420,000 according to local estate agents. While he still loves the family home where his children grew up, the maintenance is becoming too much work for him and the bills are increasingly eating into his capital reserves. He could look at downsizing and releasing some of his equity for other uses.

For both, their homes are assets that can be factored into their plan, but provide less certainty than long-term, diversified investments.

Business

Stephen owns the graphic design business he founded. Business owner-managers and entrepreneurs naturally consider their business to be part of their long-term wealth – especially if it generates dividends or income, or they plan to sell some or all of it in the future. If this applies to you, here are some things to think about in the context of your financial plan.

The value of your business is ultimately what someone is willing to pay for it at the time you come to sell all or part of it. Assessing that value is always difficult, even with specialist help, because the typical methods of assessing comparable businesses or multiples of earnings or income can only provide quite broad ranges.

From these ranges you need to subtract any debt in the business, as well as the working capital it needs to continue to run. Both of these items can be heavily negotiated when it comes to sale time.

On the flipside, if there's more cash in the business than is needed to pay off debts and ensure working capital, that cash has real value.

The value of your business to another business or investor is often specific to them and their situation, as well – does it represent a significant strategic benefit to the purchaser or is it simply a nice addition and one of many that they might buy? The sale of a business is usually heavily dependent on market conditions and how well your business is set up for sale or investment. Processes can take time, often more time than the owner might think.

Beyond the headline valuation, there's more to think about. What are the terms of sale – for example, cash, shares in the purchaser's business or loan notes (loans with or without guarantees that they will be paid back over time)? If the business is passing to the next generation, will you instead receive a continued income stream – or hand the business on in the form of a loan, with repayments? Will there be an earn out – a period of time in which you have to deliver a certain level of performance in order to be paid out? Will you need to stay with the business post-sale or will you exit after a brief handover? What type of warranties will you be expected to make (guarantees about the state of your business) – and if these turn out not to be true, how much money might you have to repay and over what period?

From a financial planning perspective, unless you find an adviser with specialist corporate finance experience in your sector, it's unlikely they will be able to assist you with the valuation process. However, they can help you factor in what you want to use the business for: income, complete or partial exit, to pass on to the next generation or to management or employees, for example. They can also include as resources in your plan any valuation ranges you do have, along with potential timings, structures and related taxes. Unless you have a lot of certainty about your exit strategy from your business, it's usually prudent to include a lower estimate of business value and a higher estimate of the time needed to realise this value, to give you greater certainty about what can be achieved.

Risk assessment comes into play here, too. Stephen has worked hard to build his business over the last 20 years and while it has grown nicely, with four employees plus Stephen, there are still good years and not so good years. The business turns over around £500,000 and makes a profit of £100,000, in addition to the dividends he draws as salary. Having spoken to a specialist adviser, he's been given a valuation ranging between £400,000 and £700,000 – towards the higher end if the business is properly prepared for sale and, in particular, if it becomes less dependent on Stephen. As Stephen begins to think about retirement, the risk of having a significant amount of the family's wealth tied up in the business begins to weigh more heavily on his mind.

In summary, like property, a business is an important component of a cash flow plan, but with less certainty about its risk/reward profile compared to investments such as shares. It can be built in by making some prudent assumptions.

Valuables and cherished possessions

Your adviser will want to distinguish between your liquid assets held for investment purposes – assets that can readily be sold and their value realised – and your non-liquid assets. Unless you have something like a wine or art collection bought for investment purposes (in which case you may need specialist advice), you are unlikely to want to factor your non-liquid assets into your plan. That said, if they are material they can be factored in.

Insurance

Do you have insurance policies in place to cover long-term sickness or untimely death – your own or that of a partner with whom you share your finances? This might include life insurance, income protection and critical illness cover. These reduce uncertainty in some areas of your plan and so should be factored in.

Matching your profile

> **THE VALUE OF ADVICE**
>
> 'A client of about 55 came to me with a huge ISA he'd built up over 25 years, mostly in UK shares. His risk profile had come out at level 5, but this portfolio was a level 9. At first, he said, "I'm so far ahead, who cares?" But we were able to get him to see the risks, particularly with a UK general election on the horizon. We switched him to a diversified portfolio with a more balanced risk profile and helped to protect the gains he'd made.'

Your financial plan should take into account all your investments – both the ones you might make through your adviser and any you currently hold. To make sure you're investing at the right risk level for you overall, the risk of those investments needs to be factored in.

Stephen and Sarah have agreed on a medium risk profile (5 out of 10). Despite Sarah's nervousness about investing, they do hold some investments already. As a business owner, Stephen has set up his own private pension. He also inherited some shares from his parents and has a little money in a stocks and shares ISA.

As a teacher who started before 2015, Sarah gets a public sector pension that reflects a combination of her final salary and her average earnings over her career. This will be factored into the couple's plan, but as a known quantity rather than as an investment that bears risk.

How well do their current investments match the profile they've identified? The dark green area in the diagram is their identified medium risk profile. However, of the three types of investments held, Stephen's ISA is lower risk than ideal, his shares are higher risk, and only his pension is a good match. Because Stephen holds more in shares than in his ISA, the overall profile – the average risk, taking into account the amount of money in each investment and the relationship between the investments – is higher risk than desired, so isn't the right match for the couple.

Are existing investments a good match?

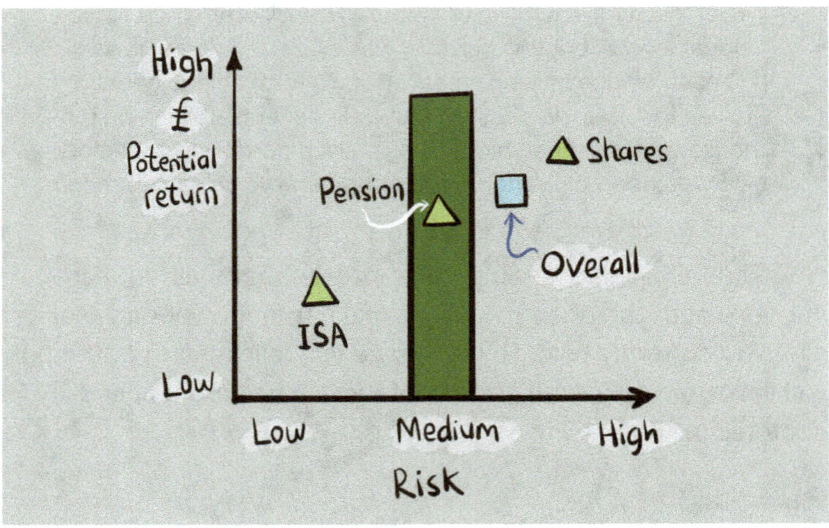

In addition to the risk they're taking, Stephen and Sarah's financial adviser also looks at the costs of the investment products they hold. Costs vary by type of investment, investment style and approach to administration. Some may also have exit penalties or charges. As we'll see later, even small differences in costs can makes a big difference to the returns you achieve over time, so their adviser will assess whether the costs of their investments represent good value, or whether better options are available elsewhere.

Takeaways

1. Begin with the end in mind. This starts with the work you did in chapter 4, reflecting on what happiness means for you and how you want to design your life phases.
2. The next step is to build a route map to take you where you want to go. In financial planning, this is known as your cash flow plan. You can use it to check in with progress over time.
3. The starting point for your plan is your current situation, resources and arrangements. To build the best possible plan, you and your adviser will need to flesh these out as much as possible.
4. Your current resources include your savings and investments, and any properties or businesses you own. Properties and businesses can be important components of a cash flow plan but can't be modelled with as much certainty as long-term, diversified investments. Nonetheless, they should be built in, with some prudent assumptions.
5. Finally, if you have any existing investments, your adviser should assess how well they match your risk profile and whether you're paying any unnecessary costs.

11. Building your plan: strategies and tactics

Having understood your current and potential future resources and the risk you're currently taking, the next task is to see what's reasonably achievable with those resources in the future.

When Stephen and Sarah look at that with their adviser, they find there's a gap between their vision of happiness and what they can afford to fund. If the same happens for you, don't despair. This is only the starting point and, as we'll see, there are lots of ways to close a gap.

What's reasonably achievable?

Stephen and Sarah's adviser initially generates a simple picture to show them what's reasonably achievable if they both stop working and take an income from their investments and pensions.

What's achievable?

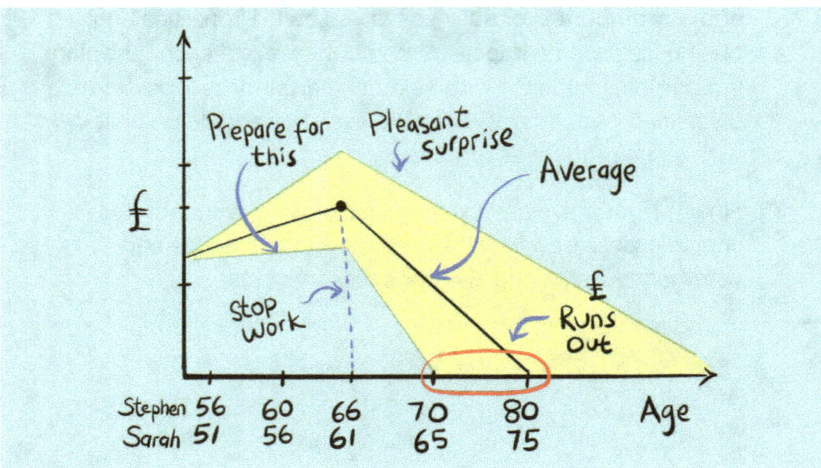

The chart at this point looks quite stark – they are, on average (the dark line in the middle of the yellow area), likely to run out of money slightly before Steven is 80 and Sarah is 75. Assuming they invest at risk level 5, as they've agreed, then they should plan for this average outcome, but should also be prepared for their money to run out five years before this.

Stephen and Sarah find this quite a wake-up call: their money could run out when Sarah is still in her late 60s – not something they want to contemplate. The chart also assumes they take an income of *a third* of what they have today – which feels like it would be a major shift in their lifestyle.

They don't need to worry yet though, because they haven't factored in their incomes and expenses so far, nor how those are likely to change in retirement. Armed with all the information they've provided, their adviser creates a more holistic picture, incorporating these resources and reflecting the life phases Stephen and Sarah mapped out in chapter 4. Importantly, this also factors in the effect of inflation – the fact that £1 today will be worth less in the future.

Mind the gap

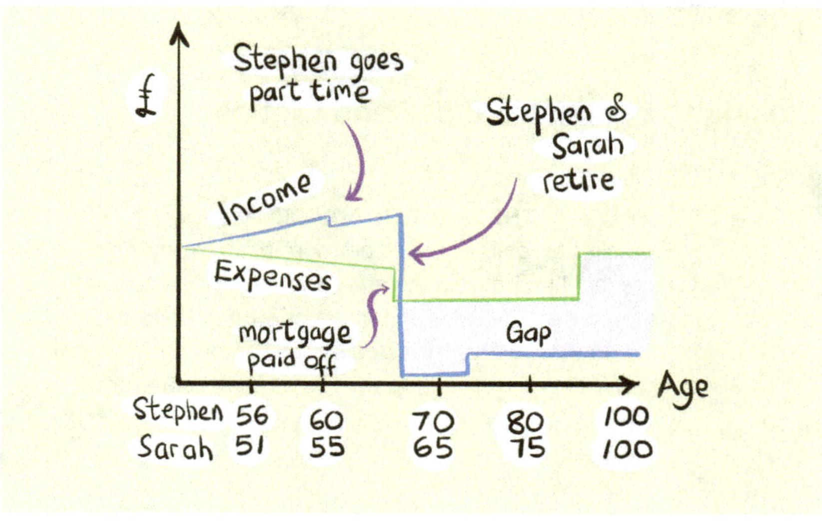

Initially, their combined incomes after tax go up, as they assume they will increase slightly ahead of inflation. The income line steps down when Stephen plans to go part time as he expects to need to reduce his dividends so the business can backfill his time with a part-time employee. Their income falls again when both Sarah and Stephen retire. A base level of income continues, though, assuming that Stephen gets a state pension when he is 67, and Sarah then gets hers when she turns 67 too, five years later. This line is straight as state pensions are assumed to grow in line with inflation. Sarah's teacher's pension kicks in at state retirement age, too, and is also linked to inflation.

Their household expenses (adjusted for inflation, like everything in this picture) fall over time, because their mortgage – a big part of their expenses – is fixed, so after inflation their payments fall in value. It's good practice to reflect the potential need for medical or care home costs in later life, so the costs take a step up again towards the end of the plan.

You can see that until they retire they have more income than expenses – so the household is actually running a surplus. After retirement, though, there's a gap between their income and expenses which needs to be closed for them to maintain their current standard of living.

Closing the gap: strategies and tactics

THE VALUE OF ADVICE

'I've seen clients realise they need more than expected to fund their ideal life. Reactions vary – some feel despondent; others become determined to make changes. For those struggling, a deep dive into their goals often helps clarify if their envisioned lifestyle truly aligns with what they value most.'

It's not unusual at all for there to be a gap between the life you want to live and the resources you have at your disposal on a first pass. The power of the cash flow planning process is that you and your adviser can use the art of the possible to build a plan that works for you and the risk you are willing and able to take.

There are a few possible strategies and tactics you can use.

Invest more. The first thing to look at is whether you can fund your vision by saving and investing more. The average household saves between 5–10%[52], but this varies significantly and, in particular, by age. Younger people (under 35) tend to save less than those in middle age (35–54) because they have lower incomes and are more likely to have debts. In middle age, people are more likely to have larger goals to save for: a house, a rainy day or education costs. Older households (55 and over) typically save the most, before moving into retirement, at which point they might start accessing those savings. As we've seen, it's not uncommon at all for older households to have to move into 'uncomfortable' levels of saving to fund their future life beyond work.

Stephen and Sarah are running a surplus currently and probably could afford to put a bit more away over the next few years – and even more if they cut back on some spending.

In chapter 4, we talked about categorising expenditure into 'must do', 'like to' and 'dream of'. If they are to fulfil their dream of Stephen going part time and then both retiring together, Stephen and Sarah recognise they might need to cut back in certain areas to their 'must do' level, so they can invest more.

Invest for longer. In chapter 6, we looked at the power of compounding and the wonder of letting time do its thing. Continuing to save and invest for longer and postponing your spending for a bit attacks the problem from both ends. Even a couple of years can make a big difference. If the goal you want to fund is retirement, this means working for longer, but if you're content in your work, that might be the simple answer to funding your future happiness.

For Stephen and Sarah, this doesn't feel like an option. Stephen has already compromised on his initial desire to stop working immediately by deciding to work a few years more and then go part time, while Sarah has a clear dream to retire with Stephen and travel more.

Take more risk. This strategy takes more thinking about. If you have a long time to invest and you won't need your money for that period, taking more risk ought, on average, to deliver you higher returns. The difference between risk level 4 and risk level 7, for example, is on average around 2.6% per year in expected returns after inflation. Compounded over time, that would make a significant difference to resources (an additional £35,000 on £100,000 invested over ten years). But remember, you shouldn't take more risk than you are comfortable with.

Stephen and Sarah have thought carefully about their risk profile with their adviser. Having looked at a few scenarios, they know they don't want to take more risk, so this approach doesn't work for them.

Achieve your goals at lower cost. This is a really interesting one and highly dependent on how clearly you can build your vision for the future life you want to fund. If you look back at the expenses you identified in chapter 4, you might see some simple changes that will mean you end up spending less. In retirement, Stephen and Sarah won't have the cost of commuting or buying work clothes. Their children will have grown up and left, so the running costs of the household will come down. Thinking through what may change based on your goals can help close the gap.

Other tactics here require a bit more creativity. Think back to the three couples on the beach in their camper vans at sunset. They were all enjoying the same experience, but at very different costs. One had rented their camper van; one had bought a second hand one; and one had bought a new one. What level of outlay do you *really* need to fund your future life?

Get creative with your other resources. Finally, reflecting on other resources you can bring to bear in your plan can help close the gap. If you own a property, can it be sold? Could you downsize to free up equity? Could you let it out full time or for holiday lets and rent a smaller place yourself to free up income? Or rent out a room? If you own a business, could it be sold or could you continue to take an income from it over time? If you don't have a business today, could you develop one – a 'side hustle' that will allow you to generate more income later or invest more now?

Stephen and Sarah see from their cash flow plan that they can get most of the way to closing the gap through saving more and making some assumptions about what they will spend in retirement. However, it still doesn't fund their 'dream of' level of travel: Sarah really wants to travel at least four times a year.

Their adviser factors in a cautious estimate for the eventual sale of Stephen's business at the point he retires. This additional lump sum after tax closes the gap completely and they finally have a plan that works.

In fact, the plan moves into surplus, opening up the question of whether they could actually afford to retire earlier. Their adviser models that for them – and, indeed, if they got a high or even mid-range estimate for Stephen's business, they could comfortably retire next year. Seeing it all mapped out helps Sarah feel better about Stephen's desire to stop working as soon as possible, and they reopen that conversation.

Plan in surplus

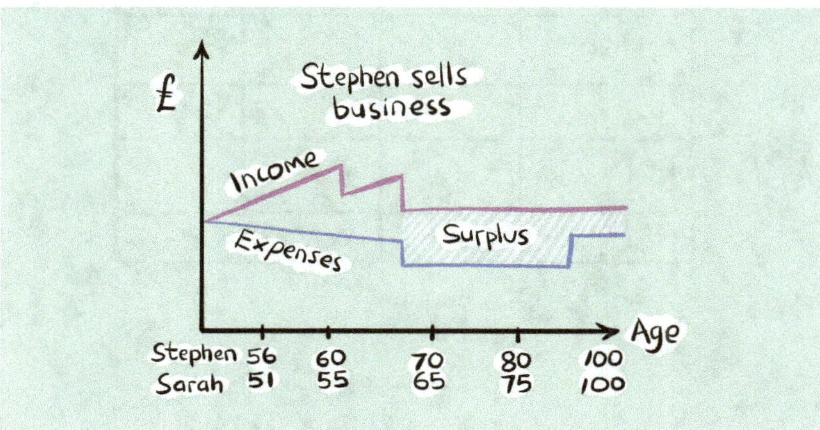

Minimising tax

A financial adviser is not an accountant – but ensuring you don't pay too much tax is still part of your personal investment strategy. Because tax only matters, in most cases, if your investment is growing or generating income, your adviser will focus on how they can deliver you the most growth or income in the first place. After this point they will think about how they can help ensure that you don't pay any unnecessary tax, both in the short and the long term.

To ensure this book stays relevant, we won't talk about tax rates or bands. The best place to get an accurate and up to date picture of taxes and tax-efficient investments is the government's website[53].

What's useful to know is that tax efficiencies can be delivered in different ways. Depending on your situation and financial plan, some routes may be better for you than others. Your money can be taxed or not at different stages of the investment process: when you make the investment, while the money is invested and/or once you take the money out.

Minimising tax

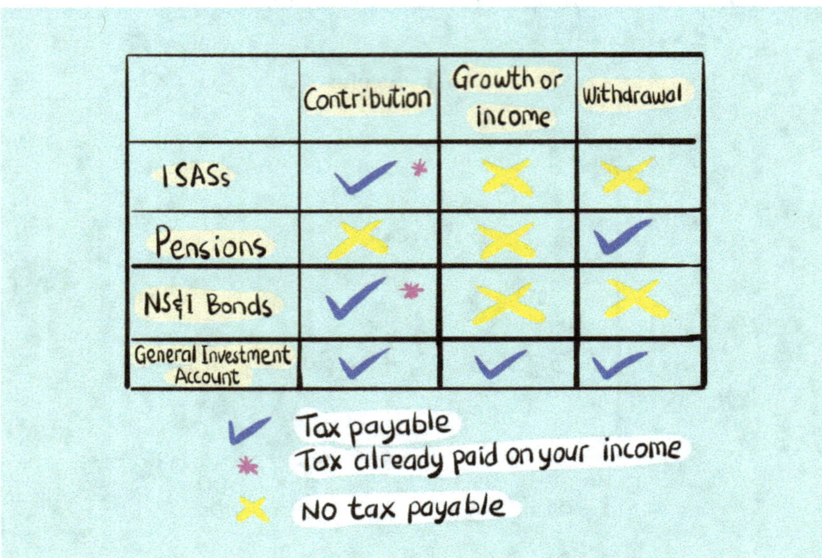

The following are common strategies and tactics to minimise the tax you pay, making use of government incentives to encourage saving and investing. This is intended as a general overview to help you have a more useful conversation with your financial adviser, and is not tax advice.

It's part of an adviser's job to stay up to date with the latest tax rules and help you plan efficiently.

Make the most of your ISA allowances

ISAs (Individual Savings Accounts) let your money grow tax free, and you don't pay tax when you take the money out. There are different types, including:

- **Cash ISAs:** For savings
- **Stocks and shares ISAs:** For investments
- **Lifetime ISAs:** Designed to help people buy their first home or save for later life

The big advantage of ISAs is that you don't pay tax on the income or capital gains (increase in value) from the investments you hold in them. That means you don't have to declare them on your tax return.

Prioritise your pension

Pensions are a powerful way to grow your money and reduce the amount of tax you pay. You get tax relief on the money you put in (and so does your employer, if you're employed). Even if you're not earning, you can still benefit from tax relief on small contributions.

When you retire and start taking money out of your pension (currently, you can do this from age 55), it counts as income and may be taxed. But this is where long-term planning can really help.

For example, Stephen and Sarah are both higher-rate taxpayers now, but expect to be in a lower tax band in retirement, so using their pensions to grow their money until that time makes a lot of sense.

Plan your withdrawals to minimise tax

When you start taking money out of your pension, you have two options:

- Take it all in one go (known as 'crystallisation')
- Keep your pension savings invested and withdraw money as needed (known as 'drawdown')

Your adviser will help you decide which approach is best for you, but in general drawdown provides the most flexibility.

When you start taking money out of your pension, you can take a lump sum (currently 25%) tax free – again, all at once or in stages.

Good planning can make a big difference to the amount of tax you pay on your income in retirement. For example, though Stephen and Sarah are higher-rate taxpayers now, combining drawdown with the tax-free portion of their pension reduces the effective tax rate of their pension income to below the lower rate.

Consider Premium Bonds for tax-free saving

If you've used your ISA and pension allowances and need a place to hold cash that's both easy access and tax efficient, National Savings & Investments Premium Bonds may be an option.

All UK residents for tax purposes can hold up to a maximum limit in these accounts, which provides monthly 'prizes' rather than an interest rate. The prizes average out to an annual prize fund rate, but you can win more or less than that average.

Consider VCTs and EIS for higher-risk investing

If you have a higher risk profile, your adviser might suggest investments such as Venture Capital Trusts (VCTs) and Enterprise Investment Scheme (EIS) to offset other income tax liabilities.

These schemes offer significant tax benefits, but invest in early-stage businesses, so they carry higher risks and aren't suitable for everyone. They're usually considered to be for more experienced investors, as a smaller part of a broader portfolio.

Manage your capital gains tax liabilities

Use your annual capital gains tax (CGT) exemption to realise gains and manage taxable amounts. There are number of helpful tactics used by advisers to minimise CGT including:

- **Bed and ISA:** Each new tax year, sell investments not sheltered in your ISA or pension up to the annual CGT allowance and then buy them back within an ISA, sheltering future growth from CGT.

- **Bed and Spouse:** Transfer investments to your spouse or civil partner to make use of their CGT allowance.

- **Dividends allowances:** Dividends held outside an ISA or pension are subject to dividend tax, but you have a tax-free dividend allowance to use each year.

Manage assets with your spouse or partner

If you're married or in a civil partnership you can transfer assets between you and your spouse without triggering CGT. If one partner has a lower tax rate than the other, it may also make sense for them to hold more of your assets in their name.

Other important considerations

> **THE VALUE OF ADVICE**
>
> 'Being able to model black swan events and the impact on their finances frequently helps people develop peace of mind.'

Protecting against misfortune

At some point in the time you're planning for, unfortunate things are likely to happen. You, your loved ones or those that depend on you financially (or that you depend on) could lose a job or business, fall ill or even die. A quality financial plan factors in these potential misfortunes. No one wants to spend time dwelling on the worst, but these things are part of life – and it's much better to think about them as part of the planning process than to have to react to them unplanned if they occur later on.

Your adviser will be able to help you though this thinking by building different scenarios into your plan. A scenario is a hypothetical situation or set of events designed to explore potential plan outcomes. Using them can help to ensure that, as far as your resources allow, your plan can handle them if they materialise.

Important scenarios to factor in are:

- **Loss of employment or business income:** In this scenario you are no longer able to generate income as expected in the plan. This may be of particular importance if there are short-term financial obligations such as mortgages and loans to be met, or financial dependents to be considered.

- **Long-term sickness or ill health:** Here, you, a partner or someone who is dependent on you is sick and is unable to generate the income expected and/or has medical costs.

- **Untimely death:** This scenario aims to ensure that your financial dependents are looked after and continuing financial obligations met in the event of your death, whether through sickness or accident.

In each of these scenarios your adviser will want to explore the potential impact on your plans and, if appropriate, whether it makes sense for you to insure yourself and/or a partner if you're planning together. For younger people, insurance can be a cost-effective option. For those in later life, insurance may be prohibitively expensive or not accessible, depending on your medical history – but it may also not be so necessary. The costs of any insurance will need to be factored into your cash flow plans.

Regardless of scenario, it's important to ensure you have a good cash buffer – an emergency fund to provide you with time to sort out the situation. The usual recommendation is enough to cover three to six months of expenses, but some advisers will recommend longer, depending on your circumstances. This money should be held in a good savings account, where it might not generate a great rate of return but will help provide you with peace of mind.

Paying down debts

If you hold higher-cost debt such as credit cards, it's usually better practice to pay these off rather than invest the money. Why? Because if you're paying, say, 20% on a credit card while only gaining 5% on your investments and you choose to invest some money rather than pay off the debt, you're losing 15% a year. If, instead, you pay off the debt, you're better off by 20% a year.

If you're younger, the argument is less clear cut. Those earlier in their careers are much more likely to have debt, but it's very good to get into the habit of long-term saving and investing at the same time – and to put more money away to benefit from the power of compounding.

Aisha, for example, does have credit card debts, along with her mortgage and student loans, but she's paying more than the minimum each month on her credit cards and has a good plan in place for getting them paid off completely. She saved enough money for her share of the mortgage deposit alongside them, and now she wants to keep the habit going by starting to invest. Technically Aisha would have more money if she paid off all her debts, but she's comfortable that this is the right choice for her.

This a good example of what's called 'mental accounting' – a term developed by the behavioural scientist Richard Thaler to describe our habit of accounting for different pots of money differently and therefore being prone to irrational decision-making in our spending and investment behaviour[54]. An example of this is holding higher credit card balances because we think of that money as somehow different to our money in the bank or money we invest. Thaler identified that if we looked at our money in the round 'rationally', we could often make better choices – although, decide for yourself whether Aisha's choice is completely irrational.

When it comes to your financial plan, your adviser can help you consider the impact on your overall wealth of paying down some or all of your debt, in comparison to the return you might reasonably expect to gain for investing at a given risk level after tax.

Above and beyond the straight financial return argument, there are other reasons for holding debt, including the opportunity cost if you did pay it down (particularly if you've borrowed the money to invest in a business or something else that could benefit you in the long run) and the need to balance present-day needs and wants with longer-term ambitions. The most important thing is your ability to meet your planned expenditure, including any emergencies, as well as your ability to pay down any debt over time.

Estate planning

As well as thinking about enjoying the rest of his retirement in comfort, George is increasingly thinking about the legacy he'll leave. For him, part of happiness is knowing that – should the worst happen – his affairs are in order, his daughter will be comfortably off, and the inheritance tax (IHT) on his estate will be minimised. All this can go into his cash flow plan.

George's adviser is unlikely to be able to provide him with the detailed legal or accounting advice needed for wills or devices such as trusts. However, she can help him understand the potential liabilities on death and – at a high level – how they can be managed. If he needs more specialist help, she may also be able to introduce him to qualified professionals with whom she has worked before.

If you're also thinking about your estate, the following to-do list should help you to plan, with your adviser:

- **Keep a clear record of what you own:** Make a list of your assets, accounts and logins so your survivors know what you hold and how to find it. Keep it safe and up to date. Using a password manager and a digital financial planning app can help.

- **Make sure your will is up to date:** It's the best way to make sure your assets are distributed according to your wishes.

- **Understand the basics of inheritance tax:** If you need detailed IHT planning, you might need a specialist, but your adviser can help you understand allowances, gifting strategies, trusts and other tax-efficient structures at a high level.

- **Nominate pension beneficiaries:** Again, make sure your money is going where you want it to.

- **Think about life insurance:** To protect any dependents if you die unexpectedly, consider life insurance. It can be used to pay off financial obligations such a credit cards, debts and mortgages (all of which have to be paid off on death), provide financial support for your dependents and cover potential IHT liabilities. Putting your policies in trust can keep them out of your estate for IHT purposes.

- **Consider gifting and charitable donations:** Both can reduce the size of your estate – and potentially lower your IHT bill. Your adviser can talk you through the high-level rules.

- **Plan ahead if you own a business (or a stake in one):** Ensuring you have key person insurance and a shareholder agreement to clarify what happens to your shares when you die. Consider shareholder protection insurance, which provides the funds for the business to buy back your shares, with the proceeds going to your estate.

Stress testing

Building a financial plan based on a range of potential returns should ensure that your overall plan stays on track, given time if needed, even if your investments go through some ups and downs or periods of low returns.

The challenge comes when multiple things go wrong at once. Perhaps the economy moves into recession, causing investments to fall in value, companies to lay off staff and the housing market to slump. Usually, as a long-term investor, you'd hope to ride this out. But if you lose your job, which you rely on for income, being forced to access your investments or equity in your home at this point would put your plan in jeopardy.

Times like this can also take a heavy physical or emotional toll. There's good evidence that being in work is good for your health[55]. The reverse is also true – and so a period of mental or physical illness in such circumstances is not as uncommon as you would think.

What can you do to stress test your plan? Here are some things to think through with your adviser.

- What if your investments fell in value to the level of '**prepare for this**' at a point in time when you needed to access them? Does your plan still work at this level? Could you minimise the level of withdrawals?

- What **other resources** would you have to draw on in order to give your investments time to recover? How long would your emergency fund last? What expenditure could you cut back on for a period?

- Could you **give yourself more time** to rebuild your income? This is all about your capacity to take risk, hence the importance of your risk profile.

- What if you or your partner **lost your source of income** – or both of you did at the same time? Again, would your emergency fund support you? Could insurance help?

These are unhappy scenarios to think through, of course, but having the discussion as part of your cash flow planning process means you're prepared. And from that comes the happiness that results from peace of mind.

Takeaways

1. Having understood your current and potential resources, the next task is to look at what's reasonably achievable. It's important to factor in inflation so you have a realistic understanding of the lifestyle your money will buy.
2. It's not uncommon for there to be a gap at first between the life you want to live and the resources you have at your disposal. Don't be disheartened.
3. Strategies and tactics to close a gap include: investing more (spending less now to fund your future); investing for longer; achieving your goals at a lower cost; taking more risk; getting creative with your resources.
4. Minimising tax will form part of your plan, both when you're growing your wealth and when you access it. This includes income taxes, capital gains tax and estate taxes.
5. Other important considerations at this stage include: ensuring your plan protects you and/or your dependents against misfortune; paying down debt versus investing; estate planning; stress testing – looking at what could go wrong and how you could manage it.

12. Building your personal investment solution

Stephen and Sarah have come a long way since that initial conversation on a Sunday evening. From feeling so far apart from each other – one of them desperate to change everything, one feeling that nothing could change – to coming up with a vision of the future they're both happy with and knowing that, if they want, they could even retire earlier.

Working with a financial adviser has brought them peace of mind and more. For Stephen, it's given him a clear path to a life he knows he wants to lead. For Sarah, it's provided her with the opportunity to focus on her own needs and wants, and in the process replaced her fear with excitement about the years ahead.

The last part of the journey is to choose the investments to get them where they want to go.

Your personal investment solution is the specific package of investments your adviser will recommend for your needs and preferences. As you will have gathered by now, this is not a book about stock picking, trading or which investment strategy is going to do better than another. Our focus is on how, in combination with your adviser, you can devise a strategy that puts you in the best position to fund the life you want at a risk that's right for you.

There's a lot of information in this chapter, but don't feel you have to take it all in, or indeed read it at all – it's another one Stephen might skip! It's designed so you can refer back to it at any time to clarify any questions you might have. Remember, your adviser knows all of this already, so you might prefer to leave it to them.

What is a personal investment solution?

An investment solution has several layers, which we'll look at in turn.

- At the heart is the investment mix, or **portfolio**: the investments chosen to put you on a path to happiness at the risk level that's right for you.
- There are tax efficiencies available to you when your investments are packaged in a **wrapper**.
- All this is typically administered through a **platform** – a system where you and your adviser can buy and sell easily and see reports on how your investments are doing.

Layers in your investment solution

Your portfolio

In the past, people who invested their money tended to do it directly – buying shares in individual companies, or individual gilts or other bonds. UK-based investors invested largely in the UK market.

Margaret Thatcher's government in the 1980s ushered in an era of mass stock market participation. Privatisations of nationalised industries and state-owned utilities were targeted at individual investors. Workplace save-as-you-earn schemes enabled employees of limited companies to buy discounted shares in their employers, while investment in UK companies was incentivised through the introduction of tax-free personal equity plans (PEPs).

Then, on 19 October 1987, came a wake-up call for investors in the UK and around the world. On what became known as Black Monday, the UK stock market suffered its biggest single-day loss in history, followed by an even bigger drop the next day, and went on to lose more than 40% of its value. The crisis sparked an understanding that this way of investing was extremely risky, leaving small investors heavily exposed to the fates of a handful of companies.

Although the direct approach still exists, the vast majority of investments today are made through collective investment schemes, often called funds. When you buy units of a fund, every pound you invest is spread across a range of investments – anything from six to 1,000 stocks – to provide you with a level of diversification that would be very difficult to achieve on your own.

Funds can be focused on one market, such as the UK, or invested globally, spreading your risk further. They may invest in a single asset class or in a range of different asset classes – known as multi-asset investing.

Whatever the approach, the aim for a fund is to deliver an agreed objective. That might be something like providing growth or income, within a specified time horizon, perhaps with some risk or sustainability parameters. Some fund objectives define risk targets for the fund (such as to stay at risk level 5), while some might specify an approach to risk taking (such as 'cautious' or 'moderate').

Your portfolio could be one fund or a combination of funds and might use single-asset class funds or multi-asset funds. Multi-asset funds might have fixed allocations to equities and bonds or might change their allocations according to the market conditions. There are infinite options for creating a portfolio; the key is to create one designed to meet your objectives, at a level of risk that's right for you, in line with your sustainability preferences.

Types of fund

There are different types of fund, all with their own features. These are the ones you're most likely to encounter.

Type	Description	Pricing
Unit trusts	Open-ended investment funds, which can issue new units or redeem (buy back) existing ones based on demand.	End of trading day
Open-ended investment companies (OEICs)	Similar to unit trusts, but structured as companies that issue shares rather than units.	End of trading day
Investment trusts	Closed-ended funds, structured as public limited companies, with a fixed number of shares in circulation from the start. The shares increase or decrease in price based on demand – so the price doesn't always reflect the value of the investments held.	Continuous throughout the trading day
Exchange-traded funds (ETFs)	Open-ended funds that are traded on stock exchanges like shares.	Continuous throughout the trading day
Real Estate Investment Trusts (REITs)	Closed-ended funds that invest in real estate and real estate-related assets.	Continuous throughout the trading day
Hedge funds	Typically aimed at sophisticated or institutional investors. They have more flexibility in their investment strategies, allowing them to pursue higher returns, albeit with potentially higher risks, including 'leveraging', or borrowing to invest.	Can be daily but more typically monthly or quarterly
Venture Capital Trusts (VCTs)	Typically aimed at sophisticated or higher risk investors. Closed-ended funds that invest in small, usually earlier stage, privately held companies. They typically provide tax benefits to incentivise investors to take higher risk.	Commonly weekly, monthly or quarterly

Funds versus model portfolios

Rather than using a fund or funds, your adviser might instead recommend what's called a model portfolio: a collection of investments put together by the adviser, their firm or an investment manager. As with a fund, in a model portfolio your money is spread across a wide range of investments that might themselves be funds or direct investments in equities and bonds. However, there are some key differences – the biggest being the tax treatment.

When the holder of any investment sells that investment at a profit, they are liable to capital gains tax (CGT) on the profit. If you invest via a fund, the fund itself is deemed to be the holder of the investments – and the fund is exempt from CGT. Instead, you pay tax on any capital gain when you sell part or all of your holding of the fund.

In a model portfolio, you are the holder of the investments. That means you're liable for CGT on any profits made when investments are sold during the life of your investment, so you can face more frequent and sometimes unexpected CGT liabilities.

In either case, CGT is only payable when gains exceed your annual allowance. You can also achieve tax efficiencies by investing in either funds or model portfolios via wrappers such as ISAs and SIPPs (self-invested personal pensions – a type of pension where you choose the investments yourself or with your adviser, with the same tax rules as any other pension).

Another difference between funds and model portfolios is the charging mechanism. Funds charge an initial fee and then a charge known as the total expense ratio (TER), which covers both the management fee and other costs of running the fund, including expenses related to buying and selling the underlying investments. The initial charge and TER are disclosed upfront, so you'll know exactly what you'll be paying in fees. Model portfolios also have a set management fee, but costs related to the underlying investments, while targeted, are not fixed, so you won't have the complete fee picture upfront.

On the flipside, because you own all the investments in a model portfolio directly, you can see fully transparent, up-to-date information on what exactly you hold. Fund reporting has a time lag and may not show all your holdings.

However, it may be more difficult for you and your adviser to evaluate the performance of a model portfolio approach. Prices for the most common funds are published daily, making it easy for you to see how your fund has done and compare it with other funds. Comparison of model portfolio performance is typically more difficult, but is improving.

A note on asset allocation

Portfolios built from single asset class funds as opposed to multi-asset funds might also have an asset allocation layer. With this approach, the adviser or an investment manager adjusts your allocation to the funds you hold and the proportion of asset classes in the portfolio over time to reflect changes in market conditions or the economic environment.

Tax-efficient wrappers

Wrappers are containers for your investments that offer tax efficiencies. They're designed to encourage people to invest and save for the future. They can be used to 'wrap' money invested in funds and/or model portfolios, as well as individual investments. Because you don't have to pay certain taxes, more of your money can benefit from the wonder of compounding when it's held inside a wrapper.

There are two main types of wrapper, each with their own annual limits on what you can invest: ISAs and SIPPs. We look at the tax efficiencies they offer in chapter 11.

Platforms

The final layer of your solution is the platform through which you invest. A platform is a one-stop shop through which your adviser can arrange for you to buy, sell and hold investments from different providers, and can access reporting about those you hold.

Advice firms tend to use one or two preferred platforms, with cost being an important factor in their selection. They typically review and complete due diligence on the platforms they use for their different types of clients at least annually.

Reflecting your investment objectives and preferences

> **THE VALUE OF ADVICE**
> "One client, a business owner, said, 'Going through the risk profiling process was helpful, but it was talking it through with you that made things clearer and made me feel less worried.'

Risk profiled versus risk targeted

The majority of multi-asset funds and model portfolios are independently certified as either 'risk profiled' or 'risk targeted'. Risk profiled means that their risk has been independently assessed, usually each quarter, based on information about the underlying individual investments supplied by the manager.

Risk-targeted investments are independently certified as staying within an agreed risk profile. This is an increasingly common way to ensure your investment remains suitable for you. The process is similar to fund risk profiling, with the difference being there is an ongoing dialogue between the manager and the independent assessor to help ensure the risk of the investment remains stable.

Risk-profiled investments can move risk profile every so often, but risk-targeted investments are designed to stay at the same risk level over time. The former gives the manager more flexibility around the risk they take to deliver returns, while the latter ensures a greater level of consistency around the risk taken.

Active versus passive investing

Back in chapter 8, we looked at the difference between passive investing, which aims to replicate a market's performance, and active investing, where an investment manager uses research to try to give you a better return.

The difference really boils down to performance and cost. A passive fund aims to give you the market return, or slightly less once costs are factored in, and is a cheaper approach. Active funds aim to beat the market, but it's rare for them to do so over the long term – particularly once their fees are taken into account[56]. However, outperformance can be more frequent over shorter timeframes, and even small amounts of additional return can make a difference over time thanks to the wonder of compounding.

Some people also prefer the comfort of knowing there's a manager's hand on the tiller, particularly when market conditions are challenging. Your adviser's firm is likely to have developed a view on the best trade-off between performance and cost for a given degree of risk and sustainability.

Growth versus income

If you're saving for retirement or another long-term goal, like Stephen, Sarah and Aisha, you need funds or investments with the ability to provide growth. If you're in retirement and need to meet regular expenses from your investments, like George does, you'll need more income-generating assets. Some investors need both income and growth – that might be true for Stephen and Sarah soon. If this applies to you, your adviser can help you to find the right balance.

Even if you're investing for growth, some of your investments might generate an income. For example, some companies in your portfolio might pay dividends, or if you're holding some bonds for diversification and to help protect your capital, they will pay a coupon (interest). If you don't need or want this income, you can opt for it to be reinvested – another way to benefit from compounding.

Funds have different share classes to meet different needs. If you're investing via a fund and you want your income to be reinvested rather than paid out, you'll need an accumulation share class. If you want your income to be paid to you, you'll need an income share class. Whichever you go for, you'll still be subject to tax on the income generated by your investments, unless you're investing through a tax-efficient wrapper.

Portfolios for growth

If your priority is growth, your investments are likely to be equity-led. That's because equities (shares) have a demonstrated ability to produce growth over the long term.

Within equities, some companies are more growth-oriented than others. These can range from large multinational companies – such as tech giants – to smaller domestic companies. Typically, these companies reinvest their profits in their businesses for future growth, rather than paying out large dividends to shareholders.

As a growth investor, you're likely to hold more of these growth stocks and less income-generating stocks. You can access them through broad global funds or through funds focused on specific regions or sizes of company – all of which have their own risk and return characteristics and correlations with other asset types.

If you're comfortable with risk and have a long time for your money to grow, your adviser might recommend an equity-only portfolio, or a multi-asset approach with a high weighting to equities. Another option is a risk-targeted approach, which aims to deliver the strongest growth while remaining within your chosen level of risk. As you get closer to retirement and it becomes more important to protect your capital, you will review your investments with your adviser and gradually move to a more cautious approach.

Portfolios for income

When you invest for income, it's typically because you've reached a stage of life in which you want investment income to replace earned income. There's more to think about at this stage than when you're investing for growth, but advisers are very experienced at helping people in retirement to generate the income they need.

As a reminder, income-generating assets include bonds, property, and dividend-paying equities, which tend to be companies such as utilities that generate a steady stream of cash flow that they pay out to their shareholders.

In retirement, you're likely to have a higher weighting to bonds, which offer greater protection of your capital and more predictable, stable income. However, most people in retirement will also need some equity investments so their money can continue to grow and their income doesn't run out. Your adviser might also recommend some property or infrastructure investments for greater diversification – or may well recommend a multi-asset solution that combines different asset classes.

There tends to be a trade-off between the level of income an asset offers and the risks both to that income and to your capital. In the same way that someone with a poor credit rating is often forced to pay a higher interest rate on a loan or mortgage, if a bond pays a higher interest rate (known as a coupon), it's likely to be because there are doubts over the issuer's creditworthiness, so they need to pay that higher coupon to attract investors.

That means there is a trade-off in your portfolio, too: between the level of income you achieve, the consistency of that income, and the degree of risk to your capital. Which of these matters most to you depends on your individual circumstances: whether you have other sources of income; the extent to which your expenses are fixed or variable; and the things you must pay for, would like to pay for and dream of being able to pay for. Look at the diagram and see if you can identify where you'd put yourself. Your adviser can help you find the right balance.

Income considerations

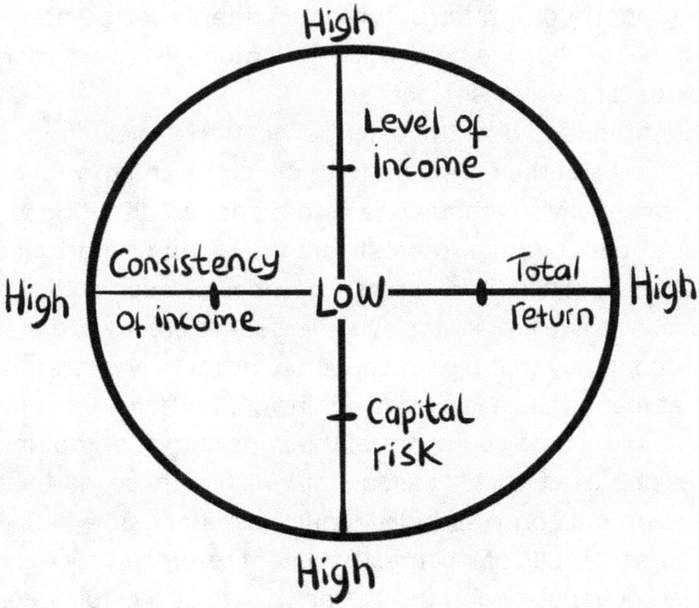

Risk-managed decumulation

A growing number of investment managers are using new forms of risk targeting for people seeking to access an income from their investments. Risk-managed decumulation (RMD) approaches aim to remain within an investor's risk profile, like risk-targeted approaches, and to limit fluctuations in value.

The goal is to minimise the impact of something known as 'sequence of returns risk' – the risk that you get a sequence of poor returns just as you start to take money out of your investments.

If this happens, you could run out of money sooner than you otherwise would with the same average return over the lifetime of your investment. RMD doesn't guarantee that it won't happen, but aims to manage the risk more tightly.

Timing of returns matters when withdrawing money

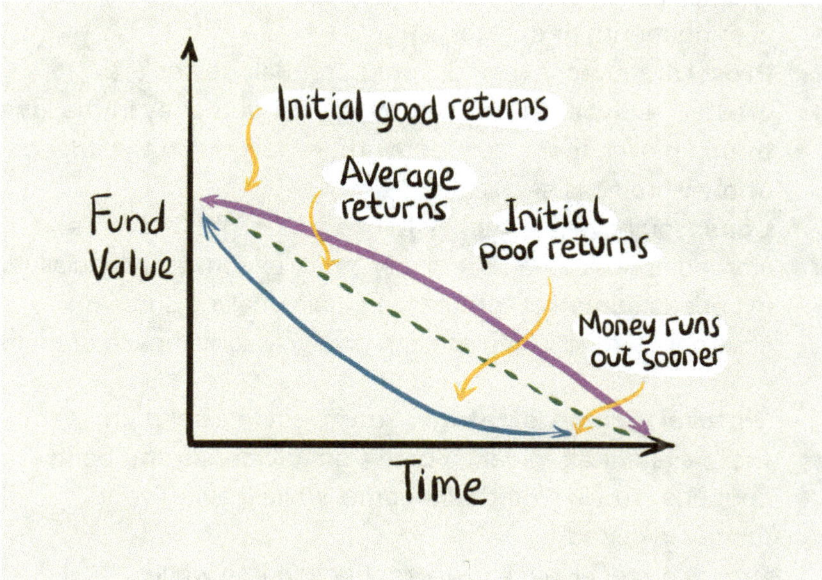

Taking your income

There are various ways to take the income from your portfolio.

- **The 'cash bucket' approach:** You take out the money you need for the next, say, six to 12 months. Everything else remains invested.
  Pros: Greater certainty in the near term: you know you have the money on hand to cover your expenses.
  Cons: You lose out on the potential investment returns on the money sitting in the bank. The size of your withdrawals means their timing can also have a big impact: if you take out a full 12 months of money after a heavy market fall, you could lock in a significant loss.

  If you choose this approach, talk to your adviser about how to mitigate this risk—perhaps you need a bigger emergency fund that will give you more flexibility about the timing of your withdrawals.

- **Staying invested and selling units:** You stay fully invested and sell fund units periodically to cover the expenses for the coming month or quarter.
  Pros: With more invested, your potential returns are greater – so you're less likely to run out of money in the long term. Smaller, more frequent withdrawals mean the impact of their timing is smaller.
  Cons: You have less money to hand, so might feel more worried about being able to meet your expenses, especially in periods of market turbulence. Again, making sure your emergency fund is in place can give you some peace of mind.

- **'Natural income' strategy:** You invest in a solution that pays out a regular income from dividends and bond coupons. You live off that income, while leaving your money invested.
  Pros: You receive a known, regular income while remaining invested.
  Cons: This approach prioritises income stability over capital stability, so the value of your capital may fluctuate more and the risk that you run out of money might be higher.

- **Guaranteed income strategy:** You use your capital to buy an annuity, which provides you with guaranteed, consistent income payments. For many decades, annuities were the only way you could access your pension, so this is a mature and competitive market. Annuities are priced individually based on the provider's view of your likely longevity. Those with health risks and therefore shorter life expectancies can expect to be offered better prices.
  Pros: You receive a known, regular income, either stable or linked to inflation. Inflation linking is more expensive but gives you greater peace of mind about covering your 'must do' costs.

Cons: By handing over your capital, you give up on the value of your investment growing. The income stream also stops on your death, unless you choose an annuity that will pay out to your partner—again, these cost more.

Reflecting sustainability preferences

As we saw in chapter 7, the ability to reflect sustainability preferences in portfolios is becoming increasingly important to investors. Most major investment managers now consider environmental, social and governance (ESG) factors as part of their investment processes, and the level of analysis has become more sophisticated, with managers able to assess potential investments on multiple dimensions.

Dimensions to assess sustainability

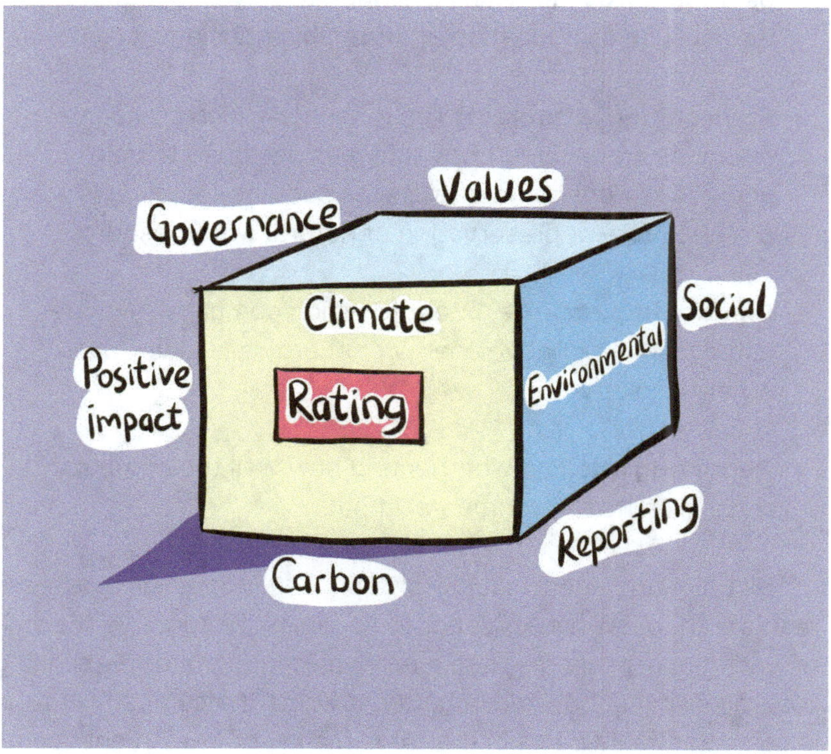

Some of the factors they might look at include:

- **Carbon intensity:** The amount of carbon used by companies (or caused to be used by companies), per million dollars of revenue.

- **Governance:** The extent to which companies invested are run based on accepted good practices such as having independent and diverse board members.

- **Values:** The extent to which the companies generate revenue from controversial activities such as weapons manufacture or tobacco production.

- **Social impact:** The extent to which company revenues are generated from activities designed to solve major social issues such as education or affordable housing.

- **Environmental impact:** The extent to which company revenues are derived from activities designed to help address key environmental issues such as sustainable forms of agriculture or preservation of natural water resources.

- **Climate impact:** The extent to which company revenues come from alternative energy or energy efficiency, plus other measures.

- **Reporting quality:** Whether and how well the company reports on its environmental impact.

Global rating agencies now also provide independent assessments of the sustainability of both companies and funds. At the time of writing, most schemes use a relative scoring system – meaning they're looking at how much better or worse the company or fund is compared to its peers in the same market or investment sector.

Multiple sustainability characteristics are aggregated into a single overall score, from 'leader' to 'laggard' (often shown as a letter or number).

Leaders can still have issues with their sustainability in the absolute sense. That said, the industry—and indeed the world—is on a journey through transition, and it's in understanding where the progress lies that investors like you can make more informed choices.

To reduce greenwashing and help simplify and clarify your choices, the FCA is introducing a rating system that investment managers can use to self-certify their funds. The system isn't a simple best-to-worst ranking, but instead it reflects the variety of approaches available. It also reflects the journey we are on, with some funds (in fact, the majority) expected to be 'improvers' or have 'mixed goals'.

- **Sustainability Focus:** These funds invest mainly in assets that focus on sustainability for people or the planet. Examples may include activities to support the production of energy, such as from solar, wind or hydrogen.

- **Sustainability Improvers:** These funds invest mainly in assets that may not be sustainable now, but aim to improve their sustainability. Examples may include investments in companies that are on a credible path to net zero by 2050, or are committed to improving social standards such as human rights.

- **Sustainability Impact:** These funds invest mainly in solutions to sustainability problems with an aim to achieve a positive impact for people or the planet. Examples may include renewable energy generation and social housing.

- **Sustainability Mixed Goals:** These funds invest mainly in a mix of assets that either focus on sustainability, aim to improve their sustainability over time, or aim to achieve a positive impact for people or the planet. Examples may include a mixture of investments from the labels above.

Advisers and their firms also have access to research and factsheets explaining how funds have been assessed from a sustainability point of view, and can share them with you for any fund they recommend.

Takeaways

1. Your adviser will recommend a diversified investment mix suited to your risk level, preferences, goals and objectives, making use of tax-efficient wrappers where possible.
2. Most multi-asset funds or portfolios are either 'risk-profiled' (independently assessed for their risk level) or 'risk-targeted' (consistently kept within an agreed risk range) to support alignment with your tolerance for risk.
3. The funds or the model portfolio in your plan can be actively or passively managed. Passive funds aim to mirror market performance at a lower cost, while active funds, though more expensive, aim to offer potential for outperformance.
4. Investments can be tailored to prioritise growth (typically equity-focused) or income (including bonds, property, dividend stocks).
5. Modern sustainable investing now allows nuanced screening across multiple dimensions, offering more sophisticated options for aligning investments with ethical preferences.

13. Building habits for happiness

Sarah's routine of checking in with the household budget on a Sunday night is a source of slight annoyance to Stephen, who can think of better things to do with his evenings than sitting there with a spreadsheet. But it's one big reason why both of them are on track for early retirement, if they choose to take it.

Aisha didn't really think about budgeting through her twenties, but when she decided to save for a house, she started controlling her spending by using pots in her banking app. She also set up a regular transfer to her Lifetime ISA on the day her salary was paid. Establishing the savings habit has helped her to get on the path to a happy retirement earlier than many of her peers.

As we've seen in previous chapters, the effect of time on your money is powerful. And small deviations, over time, can have a significant impact on your happiness, negatively or positively.

Imagine you're sailing a ship from Portsmouth to New York. A trajectory that's off by one degree would have very little impact as you left the English Channel – you'd just be a few meters off course. But maintain that difference over the whole journey and you'd end up more than 60 miles adrift!

That's why habits matter when your goal is funding happiness. Good financial habits keep you on track and drive your ability to save or manage your spending. Other habits might undermine your ability to get where you want to go.

In this chapter, we'll look at where to focus your efforts when funding the life you want to live. And we'll identify some simple things you can do to help you align your daily habits with your long-term goals. If you're already doing some or all of them, that's great. If not, you might find a few small changes will make a big difference.

Focus on what you can control

The key to staying on track is to focus on the things you can control, rather than the things you can't.

In their book *Will it Make the Boat Go Faster?*, Harriet Beveridge and Ben Hunt-Davis provide a useful way of thinking about this, which is reproduced here with the kind permission of the authors[57]. Ben was a member of the men's rowing eight that won gold at the Sydney Olympics in 2000. He and the rest of the crew attribute their success to a system of layered goals that took them from self-described 'mediocrity' to victory.

Creating an effective goal

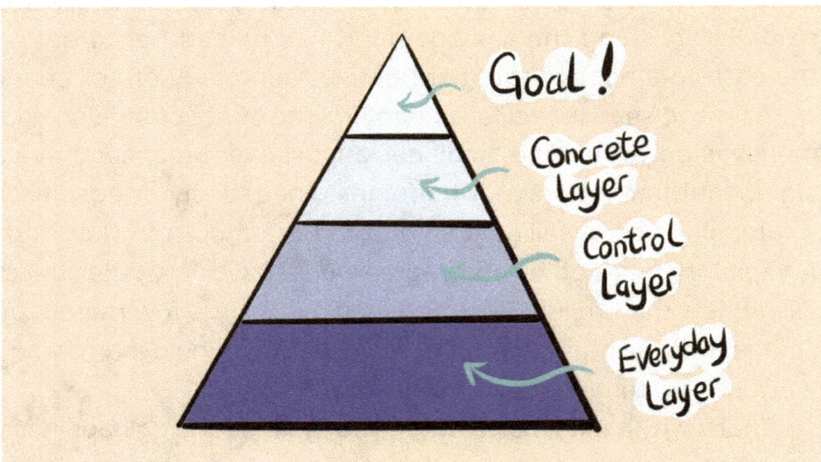

Ben and the crew had what they called a 'crazy goal' – to win Olympic gold. But a goal like that – or like funding the life you want – can feel naïve or overwhelming. To get there, you need to break it down.

First, turn the goal into something tangible – Ben and Harriet call this the 'concrete layer'. The crew set a few smaller goals they could achieve before the race that would give them the best chance of success – for example, rowing the distance at a faster-than-world record pace.

For you, the concrete layer is the plan you've made with your adviser. Your one concrete goal is to stay on track with that plan. If you do that, everything else will look after itself.

How do you make sure you stay on track? This is where focusing on the things you can control comes in. You *can* control working with an adviser, which, as we've seen, is an important step towards happiness. Working with your adviser, you *can also* control:

- The risk you take
- The amount you save or spend
- The level of protection you have in place
- The charges you pay

If all of these factors are aligned to your plan, and therefore to your long-term goals, the chances of achieving happiness are maximised.

That leaves one big thing you *can't* control:

- The performance of your investments

But if you get the rest right, with a properly stress-tested plan, you can worry about this one a lot less.

That's still a big if – and this is where your habits come in. Harriet and Ben call this the 'everyday' layer: what can you do every day to move the dial on the things that are within your control, so that you can achieve your concrete goal, and therefore your crazy one?

For the rowing eight, it was things like doing strength exercises and working on relationships with crewmates. For you, once you've sorted out your risk, level of saving or spending, charges and protections, the main area of focus on a daily basis is the tiny choices you make with your money.

Habits for happiness

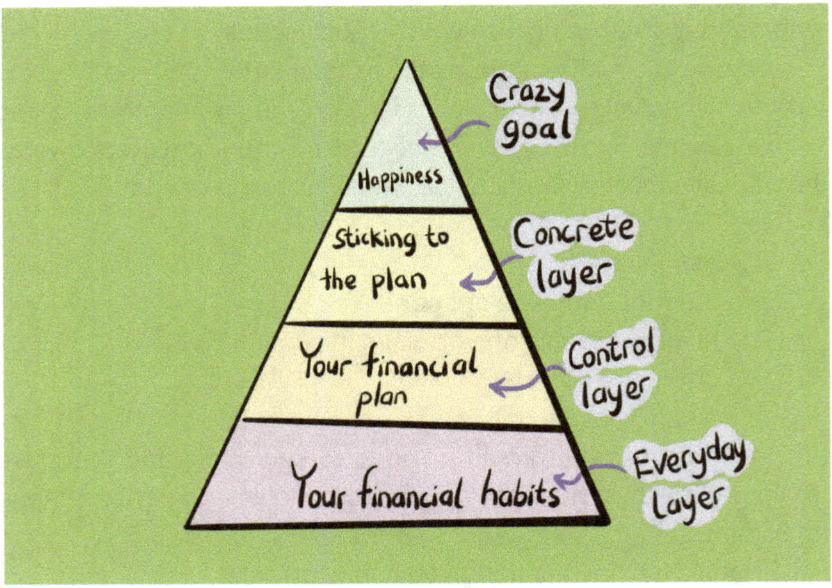

Build positive habits for spending and saving

> **THE VALUE OF ADVICE**
> 'Very often, the thing that makes a difference for a client is the realisation that they need to focus on running a much tighter budget.'

The money available for you to save is the money you don't use for other purposes. Of course, that's stating the obvious, but it's also easy to forget when you're forking out for a daily coffee or spending a bit more than you intended on a holiday.

The good news is that small changes to your spending habits can quickly increase your ability to save, meaning funding happiness might be closer than you think.

How much should you be saving?

The answer depends of course on your situation. If you are in retirement, like George, then you will probably have done your saving and instead need to focus on spending within your budget.

If you are earlier in your career, like Aisha, then saving is an important habit to build. If you're later in your career or business, like Stephen and Sarah, it's a critical one.

The old rule of thumb is the 50-30-20 rule. This states that you should use around 50% of your income for your needs: necessities such as your mortgage, bills and food. About 30% can be allocated to your discretionary spending – your wants. And 20% should be saved.

Of course, this is not feasible for everyone. Particularly early in their careers, many people find their needs amount to more than 50% of their income – this was definitely true for Aisha when she was paying rent and Sammy was in full-time childcare. But it's useful to have a think about where you are against this measure and what's possible for you.

Whether you're focused on saving or spending, good basic habits can make it a lot easier.

Make a budget

Can you fund happiness without a budget? You can try, but it will be a whole lot harder. Without a concrete plan of what you want to spend and what you want to save, you're really leaving happiness to chance.

The good news is you should have done most of the work already in chapter 4, when you looked at your current spending to identify your 'must do', 'like to' and 'dream of' costs. If not, go back and do that now, or make your own spreadsheet, or use one of the many good apps out there.

Start with what you're spending now, and then identify what's working and what isn't. What would you like your future spending to look like?

Try to be realistic. Aisha knew she was spending a lot on lunches when she was at work, but the mornings with Sammy were so hectic that it didn't feel possible to make a packed lunch every day. She decided to aim to take in a sandwich twice a week, and mostly this worked out well.

Your budget can be detailed, with tight limits set for every small spending category, or very broad brush, to allow more flexibility. What matters is that you know exactly what's coming in, what's going out, what you want to save, and what that leaves you to spend.

Look for quick wins

Looking at your current spending is likely to reveal some quick wins where you can easily cut back. Maybe you have a tendency to overspend on gifts, for example, and could set yourself a limit within which you'd still be able to buy for everyone, just not so extravagantly. Or you eat more takeaways than you intend – again, a spending limit could really help.

One area to look at in particular is your subscriptions. In a world where this payment model is used for everything from television to basic household goods, it's easy for your subscriptions to creep up without you noticing – and relatively small monthly spends can add up to a lot over a year. At one point, Stephen had five different online newspaper and magazine subscriptions and barely found time to read any of them.

Have a look at your subscriptions and determine which ones fall into the category of 'like to' rather than 'must do'. If you're spending more than you want or can afford, you could try setting a budget specifically for 'want' subscriptions, rather than assigning subscriptions to other spending categories. That way, if you decide to add in a new subscription, another one has to go.

Plan for big spends

Budgets often fall down when it comes to birthdays, holidays, household repairs or Christmas – even Sarah sometimes gets carried away.

If you recognise yourself in this, make sure you factor any upcoming events into your budget review. You could also try setting up spending pots for specific purposes and putting aside a small amount each month. That way you can spread the cost over the year, rather than letting special occasions knock you off track.

Face the tough choices

If you're overspending on a large scale, you might have to ask yourself some harder questions. Can you afford to live in such a nice house or area? Are you overstretching to fund your children's education?

These are emotive topics and the choices involved are highly personal. But failing to think about them now might mean some tougher compromises down the line.

Schedule your budget review

Your budget is not a one-and-done. Like the Chancellor of the Exchequer, you need to review it regularly to make sure it's still serving its purpose. If you're planning with a partner, like Stephen and Sarah, set aside time to do this together (even if one of you is resistant!).

It's unlikely that you'll get your budget right first time. If you're overspending in certain categories but underspending in others, that's an easy readjustment. If you're overspending across the board, that's where changing your habits comes in.

You can check in weekly or monthly. The main thing is to schedule it, make sure it's frequent enough to capture any changing needs and wants, and stick to the habit. Once you're in the swing, it won't take up much time at all.

An annual or bi-annual meeting with your adviser is then probably all that's needed to review your progress against your plan and make any adjustments as you go.

Redesign your environment

In his book *Tiny Habits*, behaviour scientist B.J. Fogg identifies our environment as vital to changing our habits[58].

Let's say I want to eat less chocolate. I currently store the chocolate on a shelf at eye level. If I move it to the back of a high shelf, behind something heavy or annoying to move, I add a little bit of friction that might stop me automatically reaching for it when a sugar craving kicks in. Even better, I could stop keeping chocolate in the house, so that if I want to eat some chocolate I have to go out and get some. I no longer need to rely on my own shaky motivation to address my habit.

Or say I find myself mindlessly scrolling the news when I'd prefer to read a book before bed. I typically charge my phone overnight – so if I move my charger cable to the kitchen, I create a prompt for myself to leave my phone downstairs and read something more enriching and more conducive to my sleep instead.

Similarly, if your route to the station takes you past your favourite coffee shop, it's more difficult to break the habit of popping in. If you always eat at expensive restaurants when you go out for dinner with your most extravagant friends, you're more likely to overspend.

Redesigning your environment means you don't have to rely on willpower alone to stop you spending more than you mean to. That could be taking a different route in the mornings, or suggesting to your friends that you give the new curry place a try. These ideas might feel simplistic, or like they won't make much difference to the big picture – but small wins can add up.

If you'd prefer one big win, though, there's a simple change you can make that will improve your financial environment dramatically: make your money, like the chocolate, less accessible. Identify what you want to save and put it out of your reach: don't leave it in your current account or an instant access saver, but choose fixed-term savings products or those with withdrawal penalties, or put it in your pension or other harder to access investment products.

Pay yourself first

Many would-be savers fall down because they plan to save what they have left over at the end of the month – but then there's nothing left. Others set specific savings targets but then something gets in the way: an unexpected expense or a purchase they can't resist. How do you make sure this doesn't happen to you? If you keep finding you're not saving what you want to save, how do you change that?

A simple habit you can put in place is to *pay yourself first*. Like Aisha, when you receive your salary or income, immediately set aside the money you want to save. Set up a standing order to move that money into your ISA or pension so you simply don't count it as money available to you. Start small if need be. The important thing is to build the saving habit. If the direct debits for your bills go out at the same time, everything left is yours to spend – without risk to your plans for the future.

Remember also to make sure you have your emergency fund in place, so that if you need to meet an unexpected cost you don't have to use money you'd otherwise have saved.

Set aside your spending money

Another approach you might prefer is to move your 'want to' money out of your current account into a separate account or a dedicated pot. Anything that's not a need gets paid for out of that pot. Alternatively, pay all bills on the first of the month, along with your savings, then the rest is yours to spend.

Save the change

Your current account provider might offer a 'save the change' facility that rounds up any purchase you make to the nearest pound and puts the difference into your chosen savings pot or account. You won't miss 27p here or 61p there – and checking what you've amassed is a good way to start feeling good about saving.

Delay your purchases

When we make impulse purchases, often what we're looking for is not the thing itself but a bit of instant gratification[59]. So if you're tempted to buy something that doesn't fit into your budget, don't tell yourself you can't have it. Instead, delay the spending by just 15 minutes. At the end of this period, you might find you don't want it at all. The need for gratification has faded, or you've found it elsewhere.

If you still make the purchase, that's fine. You're building your tolerance for waiting, and introducing some friction into the spending process, which will ultimately lead to better spending habits. Once you get into the habit of waiting 15 minutes, aim higher: wait for an hour, then a day, then perhaps a month before deciding.

Pay yourself to wait

If waiting to make large purchases feels difficult, pay yourself to do it. Pre-identify a reward that costs a small amount of money and makes you feel good. If you love reading, it could be a new book. If you value half an hour to yourself in a coffee shop with a latte, go for that.

If you have the urge to make a big purchase that will totally blow your budget, wait at least a day. If you manage to hold off for those 24 hours – even if you make the purchase after the day has passed – pay yourself for waiting with the reward you identified. It's all about introducing friction and forming better long-term habits.

Keep the future in mind

Behavioural research shows we find it hard to connect with our future selves, which is why we tend to prioritise short-term gratification over our long-term goals[60]. Building a sense of connection with the future is positive both for our overall health and wellbeing and for our ability to save.

Checking in with your cash flow plan and the goals you listed there can help you to connect with the future by showing you the journey from here to there.

Whatever approach you use, it's important to keep your ultimate, crazy goal of funding happiness in sight. Beveridge and Hunt-Davis write that all the layers of your goal are important for it to be effective, because 'without passion, a goal becomes a chore'. So don't forget to stop and look up from time to time to think about why you're doing all this. Visualising happiness on a regular basis – whether it's that camper van on the beach or more time with your family – will help to keep you on track. Many of the top performers from all different fields – sports, medicine, the military, wealth management – take time each day to reflect on their long-term goals, the progress they've made towards them that day and the two or three things they will do tomorrow that will help them progress further[61].

Investing itself might not always give you satisfaction, but looking at the money you've put into your investments will. Looking at the amount you've paid off on any debts will. Each month, along with your budget review, look back at the positive progress you've made.

B.J. Fogg believes small celebrations are key to hardwiring new habits. When we notice something we've done well and congratulate ourselves for that, we activate the reward circuitry of our brains, helping to reinforce the positive behaviour. If you like the sound of this, *Tiny Habits* includes 100 celebration ideas.

Did you stay within your budget for the week or month? Pay off some of a debt? Save or invest the amount you committed? Avoid a purchase that almost derailed you? Delay a purchase for even 15 minutes? Take a moment to celebrate that win.

Spending and saving habits checklist

<table>
<tr><td rowspan="2">Getting started</td><td rowspan="2">• Make a budget
• Look for quick wins
• Plan for big spends
• Face the tough choices
• Redesign your environment</td><td>Monthly</td></tr>
<tr><td rowspan="3">• Pay yourself first
OR
• Set aside your spending money
• Review your budget
• Review your progress
• Celebrate your successes
• Visualise your goals
• Check in against your plan</td></tr>
<tr><td>Daily</td><td>• Delay your purchases
• Pay yourself to wait
• Save the change</td></tr>
<tr><td rowspan="3">Weekly</td><td rowspan="3">• Review your budget
• Review your progress
• Celebrate your successes
• Visualise your goals</td></tr>
<tr><td>Annual/six-monthly</td></tr>
<tr><td>• Review your progress with your adviser</td></tr>
</table>

Check in against your plan

If you've ever weighed yourself regularly, you'll know that your weight fluctuates – sometimes quite significantly – depending on all sorts of things: the amount of exercise you've done, what you've eaten, the amount of liquid you've drunk, the time of day. It's only over time that a trend emerges.

The same is true of your investments. Some days they'll be up, some days they'll be down: that doesn't matter. Your plan for happiness allows for those fluctuations. Your true return only materialises over time – not weeks or months, but years. Looking back over a year, or over three years, you can begin to identify a pattern. But if you're a long-term investor, it's only really over five years and more that you should expect to see a trend emerging.

Does that mean you shouldn't check in? Not at all. Checking on your investments helps you to feel engaged with your money. You might find it motivates you to save more.

But instead of looking at your returns in isolation, look at them in the context of your long-term plan. Are you on track to achieve your goals? Is the performance of your investments in line with your agreed risk profile? If so, the ups and downs are beside the point.

Your adviser can help you to understand the range within which your investments can be expected to fluctuate, depending on your risk profile. How often should you check in? That's up to you. Try to notice what feels good and helps you to stay focused on funding happiness.

Habits in a crisis

Good financial habits help your everyday choices to contribute to your long-term goals. But sometimes a day is out of the ordinary – whether because of global factors that affect everyone or personal factors that affect you. How you handle those days is also important to your happiness.

Stay the course
History shows us that markets recover after periods of crisis. The best thing to do, therefore, is to stay the course. If you sell your investments when markets are low, you lock in your losses. Instead, wait it out. As long as your portfolio is being managed in line with the risk profile you agreed with your adviser, you should not lose more than you can afford.

Trust the process
Your plan should factor in the ups and downs of markets, and even allow for periods in which markets don't behave in normal ways. If you're reviewing your portfolio in a crisis, remember that the question is not 'How did my investments perform when the news broke?' but 'Am I on track for happiness?' If you are, that's great. If not…

Lean on your adviser
In a crisis, as in normal times, working with an adviser is a positive habit, because you have someone you already know and trust to lean on for support. If you need reassurance in a market crisis, ask for help. And if something changes in your personal circumstances that will affect your ability to fund happiness, let your adviser know.

Remember, as we've seen throughout the book, there are many paths to achieving happiness. Whatever the crisis, your adviser is there to help you to think through your choices.

Takeaways

1. Funding happiness starts with defining clear long-term goals and working with your adviser to create a plan that keeps you aligned.
2. Small changes in spending and saving can make a big difference, helping you gradually work towards larger goals.
3. Make budgeting a regular activity to ensure it aligns with your changing needs. Adjust your budget as needed to accommodate big expenses, enable quick savings wins and make tough choices when necessary.
4. Redesign your surroundings—for example, pay yourself first and keep savings in harder-to-access accounts. Limiting accessible spending money and reducing impulse buys can improve long-term outcomes.
5. In times of crisis, avoid panicking or deviating from your plan. Trust your adviser, remember the long-term nature of investing, and stay the course to prevent locking in losses or compromising your long-term happiness.

14. Making it happen

THE VALUE OF ADVICE
'I think clients are often even more satisfied that they've got all their thoughts and feelings down than they are to find that they can hit a goal.'

By now, you've travelled a long way. Not just through the pages of this book, but through some of the most important questions you can ask yourself. What does happiness mean to me? What do I really want to fund? How much risk feels right for me and for the planet? How do I take action – not just today, but consistently over time?

You've met Sarah, Stephen, Aisha and George – characters whose challenges and aspirations hopefully have helped you reflect on your own. And you've seen how advice, when done well, can help resolve the Investor's Dilemma: the conflict between wanting to fund a better future and being afraid to take the necessary risk to achieve it.

This final chapter brings everything together and gives you a clear next step.

You can fund the life you want – if you're clear about what that life is.

The first step we took was to define what happiness means for you. As we saw with George, Sarah, Stephen and Aisha, it's not just about money, and it's certainly not just about investments or financial products. It's about time, freedom, safety, purpose, connection. That's why the right question isn't 'How much money do I need?' but rather, 'What am I trying to fund?'

Working through the right questions in the right order, with a skilled adviser, can transform everything. It turns vague hopes into clear goals, and clear goals into actionable plans.

Risk isn't the enemy. It's a means to a more fulfilling life.
We've seen that inflation quietly eats away at your spending power. Leaving your money in the bank might feel safe – but it actually erodes your ability to fund what matters. Investing your money isn't reckless. It's about choosing, with care, the level of risk you're willing and able to take.

Your adviser's role is to help you understand that risk, plan for it and, most importantly, stay the course.

You don't have to do it alone.
Whether you're building your plan from scratch, refining your investments or adjusting your spending habits, you'll make more progress, with more confidence, when you're supported. That's where a great financial adviser makes all the difference.

An adviser isn't just there to recommend products. They're your coach, your sounding board, and your partner in funding a life that feels right to you. They bring expertise in planning, tax and investing, and the objectivity to help you make better decisions, when times are good and when they're hard.

Good advice is more accessible than ever.
Increasingly, advice is available through video calls or even online only, in formats and at costs that suit more people.

Don't let any outdated perceptions about advice put you off. Most firms offer a free initial consultation and a range of services, from one-off help with investing a lump sum to full wealth management. There is almost certainly an adviser and a model that fits your needs.

This is the start, not the end.

You now know the five essential questions to resolve the Investor's Dilemma:

1. What does happiness mean to me?
2. What does it cost to fund?
3. How much risk am I comfortable with, and can afford?
4. How can I invest sustainably and build a plan I believe in?
5. How do I stay on track?

Use these questions in conversation with your adviser. Bring this book to your next meeting. Highlight the sections that resonated. Share what you've learned about yourself and what you want. Your adviser will help you build or refine a plan that reflects your goals, values and capacity for risk.

And then, take action.

Start small. Review your savings. Clarify your goals. Make a list of what matters most. Book that meeting. Because the sooner you start, the more confident you'll feel, and the sooner you'll be able to fund the life you want.

Final thoughts

Funding happiness isn't about chasing wealth for its own sake. It's about living your life with clarity and purpose – and using your money well, for what matters to you. The lessons in this book are drawn from the experience of thousands of advisers working with over two million clients, supported by insights from leading academic studies and thinkers from around the world. These are tried and tested methods that work. With a plan in place and the right support, you can move from fear to confidence, from hesitation to progress towards the life you want.

So take that next step.

And start funding your happiness – at a risk that's right for you.

Appendix 1: Exercises for happiness

These tables are for you to use to complete the exercises from chapter 4. If you prefer, or find you need more space, you can create your own versions on paper or digitally.

1. Must do / like to / dream of

Income type	Amount now	Life phase	Amount future	Must do / like to / dream of	How often?
Expense type					

2. Life phases

My life phases	
What?	When?

3. Income and expenses for each life phase

Life phase	Full time	Part time	Charity
Dates	From ... To ...	From ... To ...	From ... To ...
Incomes			
Expenses			

4. Wheel of life

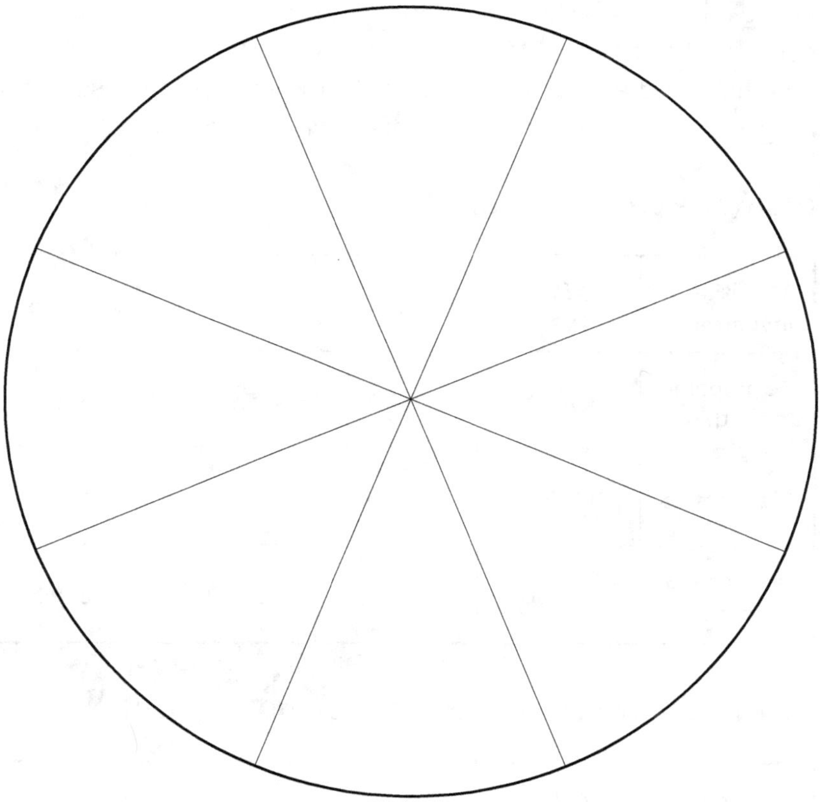

Appendix 2: Portfolio value estimates

These tables show Dynamic Planner's portfolio value estimates by risk level, based on a starting portfolio of £10,000. These change over time and are for illustration only, to give you a sense of the ranges of returns investors with different risk profiles might achieve.

Cash (Risk profile 1 out of 10)

Initial investment	After 1 year	5 years	10 years	20 years
Be prepared for this	£9,760	£8,870	£7,860	£6,180
Plan for this	£9,760	£8,870	£7,870	£6,190
Be pleasantly surprised	£9,760	£8,870	£7,870	£6,190

Low-medium risk (Risk profile 5 out of 10)

Initial investment	After 1 year	5 years	10 years	20 years
Be prepared for this	£8,740	£8,070	£8,030	£8,550
Plan for this	£10,300	£11,400	£13,000	£16,900
Be pleasantly surprised	£12,000	£16,100	£21,200	£34,200

Highest risk (Risk profile 10 out of 10)

Initial investment	After 1 year	5 years	10 years	20 years
Be prepared for this	£7,520	£6,000	£5,630	£5,740
Plan for this	£10,400	£12,400	£15,600	£23,400
Be pleasantly surprised	£14,300	£25,200	£43,100	£100,000

Acknowledgements

Funding Happiness has been a true team effort, more than two years in the making, combining unique data sets with first-hand experience from financial advisers, academic studies from around the world, and highly technical input from investment and financial planning specialists. Pulling it together has been a monumental task made possible by a very wide range of people.

First and foremost, my heartfelt thanks go to Sarah East, who has been alongside me from the very first draft, shaping, refining and rewriting every chapter with fastidious care for the impact it would have on the reader.

Thank you also to my developmental editor Laura E. Pasquale and copy editor Jenny Jacoby, and to Daud Bujang at Wud for bringing my rough sketches for the illustrations vividly to life.

I am indebted to my colleagues at Dynamic Planner for the significant amounts of new and unique data and analysis that underpin this book, and for their feedback on multiple drafts.

Particular thanks go to the many financial advisers and advice firm leaders who so generously shared their stories and provided thoughtful feedback on concepts and drafts throughout the process. The value of advice and your passion for your clients' wellbeing shines through the stories you provided.

Special thanks go, in alphabetical order, to the following people, without whom the book would not be what it is: Danby Bloch, Carla Brown, Jason Butler, Malcolm Chambers, Abhimanyu Chatterjee, Jason Dewar, Will Dunwell, Sarah Durrant, Charlotte Goodman, Tim Grey, Jim Henning, Ben Hunt-Davies, Chris Jones, George Kinder, Thorfinn Maciver, Joanne Macklin, Shelley McCarthy, Andy McGowan, Tom McGrath, Patrick Murphy, Alex Nicoley, Mark Pittachio, Keith Richards, Yasmina Siadatan, Abhishek Vethanayagam, Rowan Whittington, Steph Willcox and Louis Williams.

Finally, and importantly, I owe the biggest thanks to my wife, Jayne, and my sons, Christian, Gabriel and Raphael. You have patiently listened as I tried (and retried) endless ways of explaining ideas that the financial services industry often makes far too complicated. Thank you for humouring me, for being willing guinea pigs and for reminding me every day what happiness looks like.

Notes and references

1. Financial Conduct Authority *Investment Platforms Market Study Interim Report: Annex 5 – Model Portfolio Review* (Financial Conduct Authority, 2018)
2. 'A quiet revolution', *Financial Times* 21/22 February 2004
3. Including the Schroders 'Best independent financial planning tool' 2020, 2021, 2022, 2023 and 2024
4. Anthony Hilton, 'How fintech changed the game on dealing with risk', *Evening Standard*, 5 March 2019
5. Aristotle, *Nicomachean Ethics* (c. 325 BC) Book 1, chapter 5
6. Benjamin Franklin, *Poor Richard's Almanack* (1737)
7. Jeannine Mancini, 'Bill Gates says he's happier as a billionaire than if he were middle class - "You don't need a billion … but freedom from worry is a blessing"' Yahoo!finance, 29 April 2025 <https://finance.yahoo.com/news/bill-gates-says-hes-happier-005324753.html [accessed 15 July 2025]
8. Dynamic Planner Insights, 2024
9. Dynamic Planner Insights, 2024
10. Dynamic Planner retirement income and wellbeing research, 2024
11. Christopher Gilchrist and Danby Bloch, *The Process of Financial Planning: The Adviser's Guide: 2012/13* (UK: Taxbriefs Ltd)
12. Brad M. Barber and Terrance Odean, 'Trading is hazardous to your wealth: The common stock investment performance of individual investors', *The Journal of Finance, 55*.2 (2000), 773-806
13. Brad M. Barber and Terrance Odean, 'The Behaviour of Individual Investors', in *Handbook of the Economics of Finance*, ed. By George M Constantinides, Milton Harris and Rene M Stulz, Volume 2, Part B (Elsevier, 2013), 1533-1570 <https://doi.org/10.1016/B978-0-44-459406-8.00022-6>
14. Dalbar Inc., *Quantitative Analysis of Investor Behaviour*, Dalbar Inc (2024). Average Equity Fund Investor vs. Indexes Over 30 Years 30 Years (1/1/1994 - 31/12/ 2023). The S&P 500 Index is an unmanaged float-adjusted market capitalization-weighted index that is generally considered representative of the U.S. stock market. Other indexes may be more appropriate to benchmark your investments against. It is not possible to invest directly in an index. Data is provided for illustrative purposes only, it does not represent actual performance of any client portfolio or account and it should not be interpreted as an indication of such performance. © 2024 Index Fund Advisors, Inc. (IFA.com). Inflation $210,988, 1-year Treasury Note Index $226,982, Average Equity Fund Investor $1,009,064and S&P 500 $1,817,754.
15. Vanguard Investment Advisory Research Centre, *Putting a value on your value: Quantifying Vanguard Advisor's Alpha®* The Vanguard Group (2022)
16. Quilter, *Adviser Delta. Helping advisers to demonstrate their true value* (2019).
17. Dynamic Planner Insights, 2023
18. Daniel Kahneman and Angus Deaton, 'High income improves evaluation of life

but not emotional well-being', *Proceedings of the National Academy of Sciences,* 107.38 (2010), 16489-16493 <https://doi.org/10.1073/pnas.1011492107>

19. Wharton School of the University of Pennsylvania, 'Does more money correlate with greater happiness?' *Penn Today*, 6 March 2023 < https://penntoday.upenn.edu/news/does-more-money-correlate-greater-happiness-Penn-Princeton-research> [accessed 15 July 2023]
20. Richard J. Tunney and Richard J. E. James, 'Individual differences in decision-making: Evidence for the scarcity hypothesis from the English Longitudinal Study of Ageing', *Royal Society Open Science,* 9.220102 (2022) < https://doi.org/10.1098/rsos.220102>
21. Daniel Kahneman and Amos Tversky, 'Prospect theory: An analysis of decision under risk', *Econometrica*, 47.2 (1979), 263–291
22. Will Durant, *The Story of Philosophy: The Lives and Opinions of the World's Greatest Philosophers*, (Simon and Schuster, 1926)
23. Financial Conduct Authority, *Financial Lives 2022: Key findings from the FCA's Financial Lives May 2022 survey,* (2022) < https://www.fca.org.uk/publication/financial-lives/financial-lives-survey-2022-key-findings.pdf> [accessed 15 July 2025]
24. Statista, *Share of adults with a mortgage in the United Kingdom (UK) in 2022, by age*. Statista < https://www.statista.com/statistics/793696/adults-with-a-mortgage-by-age-uk/> [accessed 15 July 2025]
25. Yuichi Shoda, Walter Mischel and Philip K. Peake, 'Predicting adolescent cognitive and self-regulatory competencies from preschool delay of gratification: Identifying diagnostic conditions' *Developmental Psychology,* 26.6 (1990), 978–986
26. Lynda Gratton and Andrew Scott, *The 100-Year Life: Living and Working in an Age of Longevity*, (Bloomsbury, 2016)
27. Paul J. Meyer – Success Motivation Institute (SMI), 1960
28. Materials were developed by George Kinder and Kinder Institute of Life Planning and are part of a programme of trainings that lead to the Registered Life Planner® designation. George Kinder, *Life Planning for You: How to Design and Deliver the Life of Your Dreams*, (Serenity Point Press, 2014). Three questions used by kind permission of the author.
29. Chris Brooks, Ivan Sangiorgi, Carola Hillenbrand and Kevin Money, 'Experience wears the trousers: Exploring gender and attitude to financial risk' *Journal of Economic Behavior & Organization,* 163 (2019), 483–515 < https://doi.org/10.1016/j.jebo.2019.04.026>
30. Financial Conduct Authority, *Financial Lives 2022: Key findings from the FCA's Financial Lives May 2022 survey,* (2022) < https://www.fca.org.uk/publication/financial-lives/financial-lives-survey-2022-key-findings.pdf> [accessed 15 July 2025]
31. Premier League, 2022/23 season
32. Dynamic Planner Insights, Wellbeing Questionnaire. 5,000 responses (September 2024)
33. Nassim Nicholas Taleb, *The Black Swan: The Impact of the Highly Improbable* (Random House, 2007)

34. Emily Andrews and Paula Croal, 'Average Household Income, UK – Office for National Statistics', *Gov.uk* (Office for National Statistics), 2023 <http://www.ons.gov.uk/peoplepopulationandcommunity/personalandhouseholdfinances/incomeandwealth/bulletins/householddisposableincomeandinequality/financialyearending2022> [accessed 4 August 2025]
35. Dynamic Planner
36. 'Check Your State Pension Forecast.' 2016. *Gov.uk* <https://www.gov.uk/check-state-pension> [accessed 4 August 2025]
37. Dynamic Planner Insights sample of 365,000 clients, May 2025
38. Over the last 20 years, which included major stock market downturns such as the global financial crisis (2007-2008) the European sovereign debt crisis (2010-2012), the Chinese stock market crash (2015), the Brexit referendum (2016), the Covid-19 crash (2020) and the 2022 market downturn, the Dynamic Planner risk profiles have always been back in their corridors within 12 months - as measured by the MSCI Dynamic Planner series of indices.
39. Burton G. Malkiel, *A Random Walk down Wall Street: The Best Investment Guide That Money Can Buy*, 13th edn (WW Norton, 2024)
40. 'ESG Ratings & Climate Search Tool', *MSCI*. <https://www.msci.com/our-solutions/esg-investing/esg-ratings-climate-search-tool> [accessed: 06 August 2024]
41. *iea.org* <https://www.iea.org/energy-system/buildings/data-centres-and-data-transmission-networks> [accessed 4 August 2025]
42. The IPCC is the United Nations body for assessing the science related to climate change. Data and information in this section comes from IPCC, *AR6 Synthesis Report: Climate Change 2023* <https://www.ipcc.ch/report/sixth-assessment-report-cycle/>
43. Gunnar Friede, Timo Busch and Alexander Bassen, 'ESG and Financial Performance: Aggregated Evidence from More than 2000 Empirical Studies', *Journal of Sustainable Finance & Investment*, 5.4 (2015) pp. 210–33, doi: 10.1080/20430795.2015.1118917
44. Gary P. Brinson, L. Randolph Hood, Gilbert L. Beebower, 'Determinants of Portfolio Performance' and 'Determinants of Portfolio Performance II', *Beebower Financial Analysts Journal*, 42.4 (July–August 1986 and May/June 1991)
45. H. M. Markowitz and H. Markowitz, 'Portfolio Selection: Efficient Diversification of Investments', *The Journal of Finance* 7 (1952), pp 77–91, doi: 10.2307/2975974
46. Dynamic Planner, 2025
47. Dynamic Planner, 2025. Sample portfolios are for illustration only.
48. *Dynamicplanner.com* <http://www.dynamicplanner.com/documents/content-hub/The%20Importance%20of%20Remaining%20Invested.pdf> [accessed 4 August 2025]
49. L. R. Goldberg, 'An Alternative "Description of Personality": The Big-Five Factor Structure', *Journal of Personality and Social Psychology*, 59.6 (1990), pp. 1216–29, doi:10.1037/0022-3514.59.6.1216
50. Chris Brooks and Louis Williams, 'Investing Responsibly: What Drives Preferences for Sustainability and Do Investors Receive Appropriate Investments?', *Journal of Sustainable Finance and Accounting*, (2025), doi:10.1016/j.josfa.2025.100028

51. Nationwide house price data, adjusted for inflation. For illustrative purposes only.

52. The household saving ratio is the proportion of the household sector's total resources that are available but have not been used for consumption. 'Households (S.14): Households' Saving Ratio (per cent): Current Price: £m: SA.' (Office for National Statistics, 2005) < https://www.ons.gov.uk/economy/grossdomesticproductgdp/timeseries/dgd8/ukea > [accessed 4 August 2025]

53. 'Welcome to Gov.uk:', *Gov.uk* <https://www.gov.uk/> [accessed 4 August 2025]

54. R. H. Thaler, ,Mental Accounting Matters', *Journal of Behavioral Decision Making*, 12.3 (1999), pp. 183-206DOI: 10.1002/(SICI)1099-0771(199909)12:3<183::AID-BDM318>3.0.CO;2-F.

55. 'Health Matters: Health and Work', *Gov.uk* <https://www.gov.uk/government/publications/health-matters-health-and-work/health-matters-health-and-work> [accessed 4 August 2025]

56. There are many studies on active versus passive investing styles. One of the most widely known is SPIVA® S&P Global.

57. Harriet Beveridge and Ben Hunt-Davis, *Will it make the boat go faster? Olympic-winning strategies for everyday success* (Matador, 2020)

58. B. J. Fogg, *Tiny Habits: The Small Changes That Change Everything* (Houghton Mifflin Harcourt, 2020)

59. Rosa Isabel Rodrigues, Paula Lopes and Miguel Varela, 'Factors Affecting Impulse Buying Behavior of Consumers', *Frontiers in Psychology*, 12: 697080 (2021). <doi:10.3389/fpsyg.2021.697080>

60. H. E. Hershfield, D. G. Goldstein, W. F. Sharpe, J. Fox, L. Yeykelis, L. L. Carstensen and J. N. Bailenson, 'Increasing saving behavior through age-progressed renderings of the future self', *Journal of marketing research*, 48(SPL), S23-S37. (2011)

61. Tim Ferriss, *Tools of Titans: The Tactics, Routines, and Habits of Billionaires, Icons, and World-Class Performers* (Houghton Mifflin Harcourt, 2017)

About the author

For more than 30 years, Ben Goss has been fascinated by how people make long-term financial decisions – and how technology can help them make better ones. In a university summer job in the 1980s, he saw first-hand how investments were sold without regard for people's circumstances or ability to take risk. That experience set him on a different path.

In the late 1990s, he left his job as a strategy consultant, retrained as a financial adviser and founded the UK's first online financial advice business, pioneering automated, risk-based advice over the internet.

Today, he is cofounder and CEO of Dynamic Planner, the UK's leading digital advice platform, used by almost half of all financial advisers to support over 2 million people and certify more than £280 billion in assets. Dynamic Planner's risk model has been trusted for over 20 years, used by the regulator, and today certifies the solutions provided by more than 150 asset managers.

www.ingramcontent.com/pod-product-compliance
Lightning Source LLC
LaVergne TN
LVHW022209200926
848481LV00006B/1905
* 9 7 8 1 9 1 8 0 7 7 5 1 3 *